The Methuen Modern Plays series has always been at the forefront of modern playwriting. Since 1959, the series has reflected the most exciting developments in modern drama, making the most significant plays widely available in paperback.

The Vortex

Noël Coward was born in 1899 in Teddington, Middlesex. He made his name as a playwright with *The Vortex* (1924), in which he also appeared. His numerous other successful plays included *Fallen Angels* (1925), *Hay Fever* (1925), *Private Lives* (1933), *Design for Living* (1933), and *Blithe Spirit* (1941). During the war he wrote screenplays such as *Brief Encounter* (1944) and *This Happy Breed* (1942). In the fifties he began a new career as a cabaret entertainer. He published volumes of verse and a novel, *Pomp and Circumstance* (1960), two volumes of autobiography and four volumes of short stories: *To Step Aside* (1939), *Star Quality* (1951), *Pretty Polly Barlow* (1964) and *Bon Voyage* (1967). He was knighted in 1970 and died three years later in Jamaica.

D0433146

NOËL COWARD

The Vortex

Methuen Drama

Published by Methuen 2002

1 3 5 7 9 10 8 6 4 2

First published in 1925 by Ernest Benn as Contemporary British Dramatists
Volume 19 and republished by Heinemann in 1934 in Play Parade Vol 1. It was
published in Noël Coward Plays: 1 by Eyre Methuen Ltd in 1979.
Methuen Publishing Limited,
215 Vauxhall Bridge Road,
London SW1V 1EJ

Methuen Publishing Limited Reg. No. 3543167

A CIP catalogue record for this book
is available from the British Library.

ISBN 0 413 77309 4

Typeset by Deltatype Ltd, Birkenhead, Merseyside
Printed and bound in Great Britain by
Cox & Wyman Ltd, Reading, Berkshire

Caution

1899 16 December, Noël Pierce Coward born in Teddington, Middlesex, eldest surviving son of Arthur Coward, piano salesman and Violet (*née* Veitch). A 'brazen, odious little prodigy', his early circumstances were of refined suburban poverty.

1907 First public appearances in school and community concerts.

1908 Family moved to Battersea and took in lodgers.

1911 First professional appearance as Prince Mussel in *The Goldfish*, produced by Lila Field at the Little Theatre, and revived in same year at Crystal Palace and Royal Court Theatre. Cannard, the page-boy, in *The Great Name* at the Prince of Wales Theatre, and William in *Where the Rainbow Ends* with Charles Hawtrey's Company at the Savoy Theatre.

1912 Directed *The Daisy Chain* and stage-managed *The Prince's Bride* at Savoy in series of matinees featuring the work of the children of the *Rainbow* cast. Mushroom in *An Autumn Idyll*, ballet, Savoy.

1913 An angel (Gertrude Lawrence was another) in Basil Dean's production of *Hannele*. Slightly in *Peter Pan*, Duke of York's.

1914 Toured in *Peter Pan*. Collaborated with fellow performer Esmé Wynne on songs, sketches, and short stories – 'beastly little whimsies'.

1915 Admitted to sanatorium for tuberculosis.

1916 Five-month tour as Charley in *Charley's Aunt*. Walk-on in *The Best of Luck*, Drury Lane. Wrote first full-length song, 'Forbidden Fruit'. Basil Pycroft in *The Light Blues*, produced by Robert Courtneidge, with daughter Cicely also in cast, Shaftesbury. Short spell as dancer at Elysée Restaurant (subsequently the Café de Paris). Jack Morrison in *The Happy Family*, Prince of Wales.

1917 'Boy pushing barrow' in D.W. Griffith's film *Hearts of the World*. Co-author with Esmé Wynne of one-acter *Ida Collaborates*, Theatre Royal, Aldershot. Ripley Guildford in *The Saving Grace*, with Charles Hawtrey, 'who . . . taught me many points of comedy acting', Garrick. Family moved to Pimlico and re-opened boarding house.

1918 Called-up for army. Medical discharge after nine months. Wrote unpublished novels *Cats and Dogs* (loosely based on Shaw's *You Never Can Tell*) and the unfinished *Cherry Pan* ('dealing in a whimsical vein with the adventures of a daughter of Pan'), and lyrics for Darewski and Joel, including 'When You Come Home on Leave' and 'Peter Pan'. Also composed 'Tamarisk Town'. Sold short stories to magazines. Wrote plays *The Rat Trap*, *The Last Trick* (unproduced) and *The Impossible Wife* (unproduced). Courtenay Borner in *Scandal*, Strand. *Woman and Whiskey* (co-author Esmé Wynne) produced at Wimbledon Theatre.

1919 Ralph in *The Knight of the Burning Pestle*, Birmingham Repertory, played with 'a stubborn Mayfair distinction' demonstrating a 'total lack of understanding of the play'. Collaborated on *Crissa*, an opera, with Esmé Wynne and Max Darwski (unproduced). Wrote *I'll Leave It to You*.

1920 Bobbie Dermott in *I'll Leave It to You*, New Theatre. Wrote play *Barriers Down* (unproduced). *I'll Leave It to You* published, London.

1921 On holiday in Alassio, met Gladys Calthrop for the first time. Clay Collins in American farce *Polly with a Past*: during the run 'songs, sketches, and plays were bursting out of me'. Wrote *The Young Idea*, *Sirocco*, and *The Better Half*. First visit to New York, and sold parts of *A Withered Nosegay* to *Vanity Fair* and short-story adaptation of *I'll Leave It to You* to *Metropolitan*. House-guest of Laurette Taylor and Hartley Manners, whose family rows inspired the Bliss household in *Hay Fever*.

1922 *Bottles and Bones* (sketch) produced in benefit for Newspaper Press Fund, Drury Lane. *The Better Half* produced in 'grand guignol' season, Little Theatre. Started work on songs and sketches for *London Calling!* Adapted Louise Verneuil's *Pour avoir Adrienne* (unproduced). Wrote *The Queen Was in the Parlour* and *Mild Oats*.

1923 Sholto Brent in *The Young Idea*, Savoy. Juvenile lead in *London Calling!* Wrote *Weatherwise*, *Fallen Angels*, and *The Vortex*.

1924 Wrote *Hay Fever* (which Marie Tempest at first refused to do, feeling it was 'too light and plotless and generally lacking in action') and *Easy Virtue*. Nicky Lancaster in *The Vortex*, produced at Everyman by Norman MacDermott.

1925 Established as a social and theatrical celebrity. Wrote *On with the Dance* with London opening in spring followed by *Fallen*

Angels and *Hay Fever*. *Hay Fever* and *Easy Virtue* produced, New York. Wrote silent screen titles for Gainsborough Films.

1926 Toured USA in *The Vortex*. Wrote *This Was a Man*, refused a licence by Lord Chamberlain but produced in New York (1926), Berlin (1927), and Paris (1928). *Easy Virtue, The Queen Was in the Parlour*, and *The Rat Trap* produced, London. Played Lewis Dodd in *The Constant Nymph*, directed by Basil Dean. Wrote *Semi-Monde* and *The Marquise*. Bought Goldenhurst Farm, Kent, as country home. Sailed for Hong Kong on holiday but trip broken in Honolulu by nervous breakdown.

1927 *The Marquise* opened in London while Coward was still in Hawaii, and *The Marquise* and *Fallen Angels* produced, New York. Finished writing *Home Chat*. *Sirocco* revised after discussions with Basil Dean and produced, London.

1928 Clark Storey in Behrman's *The Second Man*, directed by Dean. Gainsborough Films productions of *The Queen Was in the Parlour, The Vortex* (starring Ivor Novello), and *Easy Virtue* (directed by Alfred Hitchcock) released – but only the latter, freely adapted, a success. *This Year of Grace!* produced, London, and with Coward directing and in cast, New York. Made first recording, featuring numbers from this show. Wrote *Concerto* for Gainsborough Films, intended for Ivor Novello, but never produced. Started writing *Bitter-Sweet*.

1929 Played in *This Year of Grace!* (USA) until spring. Directed *Bitter-Sweet*, London and New York. Set off on travelling holiday in Far East.

1930 On travels wrote *Private Lives* (1929) and song 'Mad Dogs and Englishmen', the latter on the road from Hanoi to Saigon. In Singapore joined the Quaints, company of strolling English players, as Stanhope for three performances of *Journey's End*. On voyage home wrote *Post-Mortem*, which was 'similar to my performance as Stanhope: confused, under-rehearsed and hysterical'. Directed and played Elyot Chase in *Private Lives*, London, and Fred in *Some Other Private Lives*. Started writing *Cavalcade* and unfinished novel *Julian Kane*.

1931 Elyot Chase in New York production of *Private Lives*. Directed *Cavalcade*, London. Film of *Private Lives* produced by MGM. Set off on trip to South America.

1932 On travels wrote *Design for Living* (hearing that Alfred Lung and Lynn Fontanne finally free to work with him) and material for new revue including songs 'Mad about the Boy', 'Children of the Ritz' and 'The Party's Over Now'. Produced in London as

Words and Music, with book, music, and lyrics exclusively by Coward and directed by him. The short-lived Noël Coward Company, independent company which enjoyed his support, toured UK with *Private Lives*, *Hay Fever*, *Fallen Angels*, and *The Vortex*.

1933 Directed *Design for Living*, New York, and played Leo. Films of *Cavalcade*, *To-Night Is Ours* (remake of *The Queen Was in the Parlour*), and *Bitter-Sweet* released. Directed London revival of *Hay Fever*. Wrote *Conversation Piece* as vehicle for Yvonne Printemps, and hit song 'Mrs Worthington'.

1934 Directed *Conversation Piece* in London and played Paul. Cut links with C. B. Cochran and formed own management in partnership with John C. Wilson. Appointed President of the Actors' Orphanage, in which he invested great personal commitment until resignation in 1956. Directed Kaufman and Ferber's *Theatre Royal*, Lyric, and Behrman's *Biography*, Globe. Film of *Design for Living* released, London. *Conversation Piece* opened, New York. Started writing autobiography, *Present Indicative*. Wrote *Point Valaine*.

1935 Directed *Point Valaine*, New York. Played lead in film *The Scoundrel* (Astoria Studios, New York). Wrote *To-Night at 8.30*.

1936 Directed and played in *To-Night at 8.30*, London and New York. Directed *Mademoiselle* by Jacques Deval, Wyndham's.

1937 Played in *To-Night at 8.30*, New York, until second breakdown in health in March. Directed (and subsequently disowned) Gerald Savory's *George and Margaret*, New York. Wrote *Operette*, with hit song 'The Stately Homes of England'. *Present Indicative* published, London and New York.

1938 Directed *Operette*, London. *Words and Music* revised for American production as *Set to Music*. Appointed adviser to newly-formed Royal Naval Film Corporation.

1939 Directed New York production of *Set to Music*. Visited Soviet Union and Scandinavia. Wrote *Present Laughter* and *This Happy Breed*: rehearsals stopped by declaration of war. Wrote for revue *All Clear*, London. Appointed to head Bureau of Propaganda in Paris, to liaise with French Ministry of Information, headed by Jean Giraudoux and André Maurois. This posting prompted speculative attacks in the press, prevented by wartime secrecy from getting a clear statement of the exact nature of his work (in fact unexceptional and routine). Troop concert in Arras with Maurice Chevalier. *To Step Aside* (short story collection) published.

1940   Increasingly 'oppressed and irritated by the Paris routine'. Visits USA to report on American isolationism and attitudes to war in Europe. Return to Paris prevented by German invasion. Returned to USA to do propaganda work for Ministry of Information. Propaganda tour of Australia and New Zealand, and fund-raising for war charities. Wrote play *Time Remembered* (unproduced).

1941   Mounting press attacks in England because of time spent allegedly avoiding danger and discomfort of Home Front. Wrote *Blithe Spirit*, produced in London (with Coward directing) and New York. MGM film of *Bitter-Sweet* (which Coward found 'vulgar' and 'lacking in taste') released, London. Wrote screenplay for *In Which We Serve*, based on the sinking of HMS Kelly. Wrote songs including 'London Pride', 'Could You Please Oblige Us with a Bren Gun?', and 'Imagine the Duchess's Feelings'.

1942   Produced and co-directed (with David Lean) *In Which We Serve*, and appeared as Captain Kinross (Coward considered the film 'an accurate and sincere tribute to the Royal Navy'). Played in countrywide tour of *Blithe Spirit*, *Present Laughter*, and *This Happy Breed*, and gave hospital and factory concerts. MGM film of *We Were Dancing* released.

1943   Played Garry Essendine in London production of *Present Laughter* and Frank Gibbons in *This Happy Breed*. Produced *This Happy Breed* for Two Cities Films. Wrote 'Don't Let's Be Beastly to the Germans', first sung on BBC Radio (then banned on grounds of lines 'that Goebbels might twist'). Four-month tour of Middle East to entertain troops.

1944   February–September, toured South Africa, Burma, India, and Ceylon. Troop concerts in France and 'Stage Door Canteen Concert' in London. Screenplay of *Still Life*, as *Brief Encounter*. *Middle East Diary*, an account of his 1943 tour, published, London and New York – where a reference to 'mournful little boys from Brooklyn' inspired formation of a lobby for the 'Prevention of Noël Coward Re-entering America'.

1945   *Sigh No More*, with hit song 'Matelot', completed and produced, London. Started work on *Pacific 1860*. Film of *Brief Encounter* released.

1946   Started writing 'Peace in Our Time'. Directed *Pacific 1860*, London.

1947   Gary Essendine in London revival of *Present Laughter*. Supervised production of 'Peace in Our Time'. *Point Valaine* produced,

London. Directed American revival of *To-Night at 8.30*. Wrote *Long Island Sound* (unproduced).

1948   Replaced Graham Payn briefly in American tour of *To-Night at 8.30*, his last stage appearance with Gertrude Lawrence. Wrote screenplay for Gainsborough film of *The Astonished Heart*. Max Aramont in *Joyeux Chagrins* (French production of *Present Laughter*). Built house at Blue Harbour, Jamaica.

1949   Christian Faber in film of *The Astonished Heart*. Wrote *Ace of Clubs* and *Home and Colonial* (produced as *Island Fling* in USA and *South Sea Bubble* in UK).

1950   Directed *Ace of Clubs*, London. Wrote *Star Quality* (short stories) and *Relative Values*.

1951   Deaths of Ivor Novello and C. B. Cochran. Paintings included in charity exhibition in London. Wrote *Quadrille*. One-night concert at Theatre Royal, Brighton, followed by season at Café de Paris, London, and beginning of new career as leading cabaret entertainer. Directed *Relative Values*, London, which restored his reputation as a playwright after run of post-war flops. *Island Fling* produced, USA.

1952   Charity cabaret with Mary Martin at Café de Paris for Actors' Orphanage. June cabaret season at Café de Paris. Directed *Quadrille*, London. 'Red Peppers', *Fumed Oak*, and *Ways and Means* (from *To-Night at 8.30*) filmed as *Meet Me To-Night*. September, death of Gertrude Lawrence: 'no one I have ever known, however brilliant . . . has contributed quite what she contributed to my work'.

1953   Completed second volume of autobiography, *Future Indefinite*. King Magnus in Shaw's *The Apple Cart*. Cabaret at Café de Paris, again 'a triumphant success'. Wrote *After the Ball*.

1954   *After the Ball* produced, UK. July, mother died. September, cabaret season at Café de Paris. November, Royal Command Performance, London Palladium. Wrote *Nude With Violin*.

1955   June, opened in cabaret for season at Desert Inn, Las Vegas, and enjoyed 'one of the most sensational successes of my career'. Played Hesketh-Baggott in film of *Around the World in Eighty Days*, for which he wrote own dialogue. October, directed and appeared with Mary Martin in TV spectacular *Together with Music* for CBS, New York. Revised *South Sea Bubble*.

1956   Charles Condomine in television production of *Blithe Spirit*, for CBS, Hollywood. For tax reasons took up Bermuda residency. Resigned from presidency of the Actors' Orphanage. *South Sea*

Bubble produced, London. Directed and played part of Frank Gibbons in television production of *This Happy Breed* for CBS, New York. Co-directed *Nude With Violin* with John Gielgud (Eire and UK), opening to press attacks on Coward's decision to live abroad. Wrote play *Volcano* (unproduced).

1957   Directed and played Sebastien in *Nude With Violin*, New York. *Nude With Violin* published, London.

1958   Played Gary Essendine in *Present Laughter* alternating with *Nude With Violin* on US West Coast tour. Wrote ballet *London Morning* for London Festival Ballet. Wrote *Look After Lulu!*

1959   *Look After Lulu!* produced, New York, and by English Stage Company at Royal Court, London. Film roles of Hawthorne in *Our Man in Havana* and ex-King of Anatolia in *Surprise Package*. *London Morning* produced by London Festival Ballet. Sold home in Bermuda and took up Swiss residency. Wrote *Waiting in the Wings*.

1960   *Waiting in the Wings* produced, Eire and UK. *Pomp and Circumstance* (novel) published, London and New York.

1961   Alec Harvey in television production of *Brief Encounter* for NBC, USA. Directed American production of *Sail Away*. *Waiting in the Wings* published, New York.

1962   Wrote music and lyrics for *The Girl Who Came to Supper* (adaptation of Rattigan's *The Sleeping Prince*, previously filmed as *The Prince and the Showgirl*). *Sail Away* produced, UK.

1963   *The Girl Who Came to Supper* produced, USA. Revival of *Private Lives* at Hampstead signals renewal of interest in his work.

1964   'Supervised' production of *High Spirits*, musical adaptation of *Blithe Spirit*, Savoy. Introduced Granada TV's 'A Choice of Coward' series, which included *Present Laughter*, *Blithe Spirit*, *The Vortex*, and *Design for Living*. Directed *Hay Fever* for National Theatre, first living playwright to direct his own work there. *Pretty Polly Barlow* (short story collection) published.

1965   Played the landlord in film, *Bunny Lake is Missing*. Wrote *Suite in Three Keys*. Badly weakened by attack of amoebic dysentry contracted in Seychelles.

1966   Played in *Suite in Three Keys*, London, which taxed his health further. Started adapting his short story *Star Quality* for the stage.

1967   Caesar in TV musical version of *Androcles and the Lion* (score by Richard Rodgers), New York. Witch of Capri in film *Boom*, adaptation of Tennessee Williams's play *The Milk Train Doesn't*

Stop Here Any More. Lorn Loraine, Coward's manager, and friend for many years, died, London. Worked on new volume of autobiography, *Past Conditional*. *Bon Voyage* (short story collection) published.

1968   Played Mr Bridger, the criminal mastermind, in *The Italian Job*.

1970   Awarded knighthood in New Year's Honours List.

1971   Tony Award, USA, for Distinguished Achievement in the Theatre.

1973   26 March, died peacefully at his home in Blue Harbour, Jamaica. Buried on Firefly Hill.

INTRODUCTION

The origins of *The Vortex*, as Noël Coward later explained, lay in a chance meeting in 1923:

> A friend of mine was a guards officer who had a problem mother, a lady whose lovers were men of her son's age. One evening I was in a supper club, the Garrick Galleries I think, with my friend when his mother walked in. 'Look over there' someone said, 'at that old hag with the good-looking young man in tow!' I tried to imagine what her son must have been thinking, and the incident gave me the idea for *The Vortex*.

The play made what was then for Coward the usual unsuccessful round of managers' offices until, in 1924, Norman MacDermott took it for his Everyman Theatre in Hampstead, once a drill hall, then a playhouse and now a cinema, but dedicated at that time to the off-West End discovery of new plays and playwrights. A near-melodrama which reaches its climax in a latterday adaptation of the closet scene from *Hamlet*, with an uneasy mother–son relationship further complicated by the fact that the son takes drugs and that the whole crisis erupts during a stately weekend in the country, *The Vortex* was, for its time, a very strong play indeed and attracted the tabloid label 'dustbin drama' exactly 50 years before anyone thought of applying it to John Osborne and *Look Back in Anger*.

But the story of its first production has most of the qualities of those backstage sagas perpetrated by Hollywood in the 1930s: the theatre itself was on the verge of bankruptcy, and only saved by Noël himself persuading the novelist Michael Arlen to make them a gift of £250. Then the original leading lady, Kate Cutler, announced a week away from the first night that the part of the mother (though written by Noël with her in mind) was in fact unsuitable and that she would be leaving the cast.

In some desperation, Coward approached Lilian Braithwaite, a tall, dark grande dame of the theatre accustomed to presiding over graceful tea-party scenes in light comedies at the Haymarket. Seeing the challenge of a totally different and vastly more neurotic role, she agreed at once to step into the breach, only then to find the Lord Chamberlain threatening to deny the play a licence for performance since its theme was 'far too unpleasant', though whether this referred to the mother's nymphomania, the son's drug-addiction or his passionate devotion to his mother remained unclear. In the event, on the morning of the first night, Noël (who was himself playing the son and co-directing with MacDermott) repaired to St James's Palace and convinced the Lord Chamberlain that so far from being unpleasant, his play was in fact a moral tract of the highest order about the evils of drugs.

Beyond doubt, the play came as a severe shock to its Hampstead audience: here, from a writer of hitherto minor light comedies, was a play about drug-addiction at a time when alcoholism was still barely mentioned on the stage, and the reviews were both impressed and stunned as Noël recalled: 'Practically all of my notices for this play were generously adulatory, though most of them were concerned that I should choose such an "unpleasant" subject and such "decadent" types. I have come to the conclusion that an "unpleasant" subject is something that everybody knows about, but shrinks from the belief that other people know about it too ... The minor characters in *The Vortex* drink cocktails, employ superlatives, and sometimes turn on the gramophone ... Florence takes lovers occasionally and Nicky takes drugs very occasionally ... I consider neither of these vices are any more unpleasant than murder or seduction, both of which have been a standing tradition in the English theatre for many years.'

Yet, in fact, the first night had been nothing short of a triumph for Noël, who as author, star and co-director had still been forced to spend most of the afternoon on his hands and knees with his designer Gladys Calthrop and the Hampstead stage manager finishing off the set; he then got away with a nerve-strung, histrionic *tour de force* that in later weeks he was able to refine and discipline into a more subdued but perhaps no more effective reading of the part. Until then, by virtue of being his own director, he had not found time to do much about his acting, but the tension of his performance on opening night was increased by the fact that in sweeping a collection of bottles from a dressing-room table in the last act he managed to cut his wrist quite badly, which then bled effectively throughout his curtain speech. Blood, like children and dogs, can usually be relied on as an applause-raiser, though on this occasion the play would unquestionably have survived without it.

A fashionable audience led by the Mountbattens and what *The Tatler* called 'all the regular theatrical enthusiasts of *le beau monde*' made the then unusual trek to Hampstead on the strength of Noël's light-comedy reputation, and their reaction was much akin to that which greeted Osborne at the Court half a century later: now, and in cold print, Nicky's outburst against his mother and the depraved world around her may seem a little over the top: but on stage in 1924, without even a backward glance at Pinero, there's no doubt that it came over as very startling indeed. 'If I had written that,' said Michael Arlen going backstage after the opening, 'I should have been so very proud.'

Most critics acknowledged a kind of fashionable depravity in Nicky's drug-taking and the social gossip about the weekend house-party set to whose private lives it was widely believed that Noël already belonged: but it was left to St John Ervine among the original reviewers to realise that on the contrary *The Vortex* is a highly moral tract, dedicated to the virtues of old-fashioned hard work and clean living, and to standards by which most of the characters are tried and found wanting. Like so much of Coward's later work, right through *Post Mortem* to his last *Suite in Three Keys*, *The Vortex* is concerned with standards – with what is done and not done in the best moral code of values. One is made constantly aware here of the dignities of life and of how these are being abused: 'It doesn't matter about death', Nicky tells his mother at the end of Act Three, 'but it matters terribly about life' and, by implication, the way we choose to live it.

Reviews that were simultaneously shocked and enthusiastic, plus a public titillated by the murmur of something faintly immoral, assured for *The Vortex* a sold-out Hampstead season and a rapid transfer to the West End: the feeling was that the boy wonder, 'destiny's tot' as Woollcott was later to call him, had come up with something solid and lasting which would ensure him success as a dramatist rather more powerfully than the brittle and precarious social hits that had gone before. Eight managers put in bids for the transfer, and the one that won opened it at the Royalty in December 1924 at the start of a run lasting more than two hundred performances there and at other West End homes.

Superficially, the resemblance between Noël and Nicky Lancaster was too great for him ever to escape the 'well groomed, witty and decadent' label of the neurotic misfit that he had created for his play, but to have argued with all that publicity would have been futile and Noël was astute enough to realise that gossip columnists might find the truth about his hard-working, puritan ethic a lot less exciting. At a time when the advertising industry was still in its infancy, *The Vortex* was an early example of the image becoming the reality, and on Coward's home life its effect was electric:

> With this success came many pleasurable trappings. A car. New suits. Silk shirts. An extravagant amount of pyjamas and dressing gowns, and a still more extravagant amount of publicity. I was photographed, and interviewed, and photographed again. In the street. In the park. In my dressing room. At my piano. With my dear old mother, without my dear old mother and on one occasion sitting up in an over-elaborate bed looking like a heavily doped Chinese Illusionist. This last photograph, I believe, did me a good deal of harm. People glancing at it concluded at once, and with a certain justification, that I was undoubtedly a weedy sensualist in the last stages of physical and moral disintegration, and that they had better hurry off to see me in my play before my inevitable demise placed that faintly macabre pleasure beyond their reach. This attitude, while temporarily very good for business, became irritating after a time and for many years I was seldom mentioned in the press without allusions to 'cocktails', 'postwar hysteria' and 'decadence.'

The Royalty opening of *The Vortex* was on Noël's 25th birthday, and he made a restrained curtain speech hoping that the West

End would enjoy the play as much as had audiences up in Hampstead. This they did, though the *Daily Mail* was still writing of 'a dustbin of a play', and Agate after a good deal of praise ended his *Sunday Times* review 'the third act is too long, there is too much piano playing in the second, and ladies do not exhale cigarette smoke through their noses'. Still, the majority view was that of Ivor Brown who wrote that 'as actor and author Coward drives at reality'.

The play then became something of a *cause célèbre* when Sir Gerald du Maurier, at that time the effective leader of the acting profession in Britain, wrote a scathing attack on the immorality of modern drama in general and *The Vortex* in particular. Coward was immediately defended in print by Arnold Bennett and Edward Knoblock, but by now there was little doubt that the play had dragged the London theatre from Edwardian gentility or Barriesque whimsy towards the acid cynicism of social commentary for the first time since Wilde. Hannen Swaffer still deprecated 'the most decadent play of our time' while another critic noted ruefully that 'the fault, dear Noël, lies not in our Ma's but in ourselves that we are slaves to dope'.

The Vortex was, beyond all others, the play which typified the less attractive social characteristics of London and the mid-20's: it also achieved a footnote in theatre history as the first major production in which the cast took curtain calls only at the end of the play and not between each act as hitherto. Eventually Noël was to take his drama on to Broadway and a long American tour ('success took me to her bosom like a maternal boa constrictor') and in 1927 it was made into a silent film by Ivor Novello and Frances Doble, while Dirk Bogarde starred in a major 1952 stage revival. In 1989 Philip Prowse, as director and designer, brought a highly acclaimed revival starring Maria Aitken and Rupert Everett into the West End from the Citizens Theatre in Glasgow. Michael Grandage's production at the Donmar Warehouse in 2002 starred Chiwetel Ejiofor as Nicky and Francesca Annis as Florence Lancaster.

Sheridan Morley

THE VORTEX

Characters

The Vortex was first presented by Norman Macdermott at the Everyman Theatre, Hampstead, London, 25 November 1924. The cast was as follows:

PRESTON	CLAIRE KEEP
HELEN SAVILLE	MARY ROBSON
PAUNCEFORT QUENTIN	F. KINSEY PEILE
CLARA HIBBERT	MILLIE SIM
FLORENCE LANCASTER	LILIAN BRAITHWAITE
TOM VERYAN	ALAN HOLLIS
NICKY LANCASTER	NOËL COWARD
DAVID LANCASTER	BROMLEY DAVENPORT
BUNTY MAINWARING	MOLLY KERR
BRUCE FAIRLIGHT	IVOR BARNARD
Director	NOËL COWARD
Designer	G.E. CALTHROP
Costumes	WILLIAM CHAPPELL

The play was revived at the Donmar Warehouse opening on 10 December 2002 with the following cast:

PRESTON	TONI KANAL
HELEN SAVILLE	DEBORAH FINDLAY
PAUNCEFORT QUENTIN	BETTE BOURNE
CLARA HIBBERT	NINA SOSANYA
FLORENCE LANCASTER	FRANCESCA ANNIS
TOM VERYAN	MARK UMBERS
NICKY LANCASTER	CHIWETEL EJIOFOR
DAVID LANCASTER	MICHAEL HADLEY
BUNTY MAINWARING	INDIRA VARMA
BRUCE FAIRLIGHT	DANIEL WEYMAN
Director	MICHAEL GRANDAGE
Designer	CHRISTOPHER ORAM

ACT I

The scene is the drawing-room of MRS LANCASTER'S *flat in London. The colours and decoration are on the verge of being original. The furniture is simple but distinctly expensive.*

Persons shown are HELEN SAVILLE *and* PAUNCEFORT QUENTIN. HELEN SAVILLE *and* PAUNCEFORT QUENTIN *are shown in by* PRESTON. HELEN *is a smartly dressed woman of about thirty.* 'PAWNIE' *is an elderly maiden gentleman.*

PRESTON: I'm expecting Mrs Lancaster in at any moment now, ma'am.

HELEN: Thank you, Preston, we'll wait a little.

PRESTON: Shall I get you some tea?

HELEN: No thanks, we've already had some – give me a cigarette, Pawnie, they're in that box on the table.

PAWNIE hands her cigarette box. PRESTON *goes out.*

PAWNIE: It may be tiresome of me, but I think all this colouring is oppressive.

HELEN: You make such a 'Fetish' of house decoration, Pawnie.

PAWNIE (*wandering round the room*): Not at all, but I do like things to be good and right.

HELEN: Well, I don't consider the new frieze in your bathroom either good or right.

PAWNIE: How can you, Helen! It's too marvellous for words. Parelli designed it specially for me.

HELEN: Personally, it would make me self-conscious to sit in a bath surrounded by frisky gods and goddesses all with such better figures than mine.

PAWNIE: I find it encouraging. This whole room is so typical of Florence.

HELEN: In what way?

PAWNIE: Every way. Look at the furniture.

HELEN: A little artificial perhaps, but quite harmless.

3

PAWNIE: Dear Helen, you're such a loyal friend.

HELEN: I'm very fond of Florence.

PAWNIE: We all are. Oh, my God, look at that lamp-shade!

HELEN: I gave it to her last Christmas.

PAWNIE: Wasn't that a little naughty of you?

HELEN: I don't see why, it's extremely pretty.

PAWNIE: Too unrestrained. Such a bad example for the servants. (*He takes up frame from desk.*) Who's this boy?

HELEN: Tom Veryan. You must have seen him.

PAWNIE: Florence's past, present or future?

HELEN: Present.

PAWNIE: He has that innocent look that never fails to attract elderly women.

HELEN: Don't be a cat.

PAWNIE: I wasn't meaning Florence, she's too divine to be in any marked category.

HELEN: I wonder.

PAWNIE: Oh, yes, Helen, deathless sort of magnetism, you know.

HELEN: I often wonder what will happen to Florence eventually.

PAWNIE: My dear, I'm far too occupied in wondering what's going to happen to me to worry about other people.

HELEN: I've always thought your course was quite clear, Pawnie.

PAWNIE: However offensive that remark was intended to be, Helen, I shall take it in the most complimentary spirit.

HELEN: I'm sure you will.

PAWNIE: I expect Florence will just go on and on, then suddenly become quite beautifully old, and go on and on still more.

HELEN: It's too late now for her to become beautifully old, I'm afraid. She'll have to be young indefinitely.

PAWNIE: I don't suppose she'll mind that, but it's trying for David.

HELEN: And fiendish for Nicky.

PAWNIE: Oh, no, my dear, you're quite wrong there. I'm sure Nicky doesn't care a damn.

HELEN: It's difficult to tell with Nicky.

PAWNIE: He's divinely selfish; all amusing people are.

HELEN: Did you hear him play in Paris?

4

PAWNIE: Yes.

HELEN: Well?

PAWNIE: Erratic – one or two things perfect, but he's slovenly.

HELEN: He only takes things seriously in spurts, but still he's very young.

PAWNIE: Do you really think that's a good excuse.

HELEN: No, I'm afraid not, especially when so much depends on it.

PAWNIE: What does depend on it?

HELEN: Everything – his life's happiness.

PAWNIE: Don't be so terribly intense, dear.

HELEN: It's true.

PAWNIE: I'm quite sure Nicky will be perfectly happy as long as he goes on attracting people; he loves being attractive.

HELEN: Naturally, he's Florence's son.

PAWNIE: Such an exciting thing to be.

HELEN: You don't believe Nicky's got anything in him at all, do you?

PAWNIE (lightly): I don't think it matters, anyway.

HELEN: I do.

PAWNIE: But you've got a loving nature, Helen. I always knew it.

HELEN: Nicky hasn't had a chance.

PAWNIE: Nonsense – he's had everything he wanted ever since the day he was born, and he'll go on wasting his opportunities until he dies.

HELEN: Quite possibly.

PAWNIE: Well, there you are then.

HELEN: He may have had everything he wanted, but he's had none of the things he really needs.

PAWNIE: Are you talking socially or spiritually.

HELEN: You're quite right, Pawnie, you wouldn't be so beautifully preserved if you'd wasted any of your valuable time or sincerity.

PAWNIE: I forgive you for that, Helen, freely.

HELEN: Thank you so much.

PAWNIE: You must realise one thing, everyone is sacrificed to Florence – it's as it should be – of course, she's a couple of hundred years too late – she ought to have been a flaunting, intriguing King's mistress, with black page boys and jade baths and things too divine —

Enter PRESTON.

PRESTON (*announcing*): Miss Hibbert.

Enter CLARA HIBBERT – *she is affected, but quite well dressed.* PRESTON *goes out.*

CLARA: My *dears*. Isn't Florence back *yet*?

HELEN: No, we're waiting for her.

PAWNIE: You look harassed, Clara.

CLARA: I am harassed.

HELEN: Why?

CLARA: I'm singing to-night for Laura Tennant – she's giving a dreadful reception at her dreadful house for some dreadful Ambassador —

PAWNIE: How dreadful!

CLARA: No one will listen to me, of course – they'll all be far too busy avoiding the Cup and searching for the Champagne.

HELEN: What are you singing?

CLARA: One Gabriel Faure, two Reynaldo Hahn's and an Aria.

PAWNIE: Which Aria?

CLARA: I can't think, but my accompanist will know – I've got a frightful headache.

HELEN: Why don't you take off your hat?

CLARA: My dear, I daren't – I've just had my hair done – I suppose you haven't got a 'Cachet Faivre', either of you?

HELEN: No, but Florence has, I expect – Preston will know where they are – ring the bell, Pawnie.

PAWNIE (*ringing bell*): My poor Clara – I do hope your singing to-night will justify the fuss you're making this afternoon.

CLARA: Don't be so *brutal*, Pawnie.

HELEN: Is Gregory going with you?

CLARA: Of *course* – I *never* sing unless he's there – he gives me such marvellous moral support.

PAWNIE: 'Moral' is hardly the word *I* should have chosen, dear.

Enter PRESTON.

HELEN: Do you know if Mrs Lancaster has any 'Cachet Faivre' anywhere?

PRESTON: Yes, ma'am – I think so.

CLARA: *Do* get me one, Preston, I'm suffering *tortures*.

PRESTON: Very well, miss.

She goes out.

PAWNIE: Preston has such wonderful poise, hasn't she?

HELEN: She needs it in this house.

CLARA: I do wish Florence would hurry up. I want to borrow her green fan. I've got a new Patou frock that positively *demands* it.

HELEN: She can't be long now.

CLARA: I suppose I daren't ask Preston for the fan and creep away with it?

HELEN: I shouldn't, if I were you – Florence is very touchy over that sort of thing.

CLARA: She promised it to me ages ago.

PAWNIE: Surely there isn't such a desperate hurry? You won't be singing until about half-past eleven.

CLARA (*petulantly*): My *dear*, I've got to *rehearse* – I don't know a *word* —

Re-enter PRESTON *with a 'Cachet Faivre' and a glass of water.*

CLARA: You're a *Saint*, Preston – thank you a *thousand* times —

PAWNIE: Soak it a little first, dear, or you'll choke, and I should *detest* that.

CLARA soaks 'Cachet' and then swallows it. PRESTON *goes out.*

CLARA: Now I must lie down *flat* – get out of the way, Helen.

PAWNIE: Perhaps you'd like us *both* to go *right* out of the room and sit in the *hall*?

CLARA: No, Pawnie, I should never expect the least consideration from you.

She lies down flat on the divan, HELEN *arranges cushions for her.*

CLARA: Thank you, Helen darling – I shall always come to you whenever I'm ill.

HELEN: That *will* be nice.

Enter FLORENCE LANCASTER *followed by* TOM VERYAN. FLORENCE *is brilliantly dressed almost to the point of being 'outre'. Her face still retains the remnants of great beauty.* TOM *is athletic and good looking. One feels he is good at games and extremely bad at everything else.*

FLORENCE: Helen – Pawnie, have you been here long?

PAWNIE: No, only a few hours.

FLORENCE: My dear. I'm so frightfully sorry – we've been held up for ages in the traffic. Davis is a congenital idiot. Always manages to get to a turning just as the policeman puts out his hand. No initiative whatever. What's happened to Clara? Has she been run over?

CLARA: No, dear, I've got a frightful head.

FLORENCE: Pawnie, you know Tom, don't you? – Tom Veryan, Mr Quentin, I'm sure you'll adore one another.

TOM (*shaking hands*): How are you?

PAWNIE: Very well, thank you – how sweet of you to ask me?

FLORENCE: Is there anything I can do, Clara?

CLARA: Yes, dear, lend me your green fan for to-night.

FLORENCE: All right – but you *won't* get too carried away with it, will you, dear? I should hate the feathers to come out. Does anyone want any tea?

HELEN: No thanks, dear.

FLORENCE: Cocktails, then?

PAWNIE: It's too early.

FLORENCE (*ringing bell*): It's never too early for a cocktail.

CLARA: I should like to go quite quietly into a Convent, and never see anybody again ever —

PAWNIE: Gregory would be bored stiff in a Convent.

FLORENCE: We've just been to a most frightful Charity *matinée*. Nothing but inaudible speeches from dreary old actors, and leading ladies nudging one another all over the stage. (PRESTON *enters.*) Cocktails, Preston, and ask Barker to wrap up my green fan for Miss Hibbert to take away with her.

PRESTON: Very good, ma'am.

She goes out.

CLARA: You're an angel, Florence – I think I'll sit up now.

FLORENCE: Do, dear, then Tom will be able to sit down.

CLARA (*sitting up*): I really do feel most peculiar.

PAWNIE: You look far from normal, dear.

CLARA: If Pawnie's rude to me any more I shall burst into tears.

FLORENCE: Tom, give me a cigarette.

PAWNIE: Here are some.

FLORENCE: No, Tom has a special rather hearty kind that I adore.

CLARA: Lend me your lip stick, Helen, mine has sunk down into itself.

HELEN: Here you are.

CLARA: What a lovely colour! I look far prettier than I feel.

FLORENCE (*to* TOM): Thank you, angel.

CLARA: I shan't be able to get down to the house until Saturday evening, Florence – I'm seeing Gregory off to Newcastle.

PAWNIE: Why Newcastle?

CLARA: His home's just near there – isn't it too awful for him?

FLORENCE: Well, wire me the time of your train, won't you?

CLARA: Of course, dear.

HELEN: You're smelling divinely, Florence. What is it?

FLORENCE (*flicking her handkerchief*): It is good, isn't it?

PAWNIE: 'Narcisse Noir' of Caron, I use it.

FLORENCE: Yes, you would, Pawnie.

Re-enter PRESTON *with parcel.*

PRESTON: Here is the fan, miss.

CLARA (*taking it*): Thank you *so* much – you are sweet, Florence. A fan gives me such a feeling of *security* when I'm singing modern stuff. (PRESTON *goes out.*) I must rush now —

FLORENCE: Don't you want a cocktail before you go?

CLARA: No, darling – I should only hiccup all the evening. Good-bye, you've been *such* a comfort – good-bye, Helen – Pawnie, you will be nicer to me over the week-end, won't you? I shall be *so* depressed, what with Gregory going away and every-thing – Good-bye, Tom – I shall dine in bed and give way at every pore —

She goes out.

PAWNIE: Poor Clara – she eternally labours under the delusion that she really matters.

HELEN: We all do that a little.

FLORENCE (*laughing*): You're awfully cruel to her, Pawnie.

PAWNIE: She upsets my vibrations.

FLORENCE (*before glass*): I've taken a sudden hatred to this hat. (*She takes it off.*) That's better – are you going to *The New Elaine* to-night, either of you?

HELEN: I'm not – but Pawnie is, of course.

PAWNIE: It's going to be *amazing* – what a cast, my dear! Marvellous Selwyn Steele, Nora Dean, and that perfect woman, Lily Burfield —

HELEN: I can't stand her, she always over-acts.

PAWNIE (*incensed*): How *can* you, Helen! Did you see her in *Simple Faith*?

HELEN: Yes, unfortunately.

PAWNIE: Oh, you really are too tiresome for words!

HELEN: Her technique creaks like machinery.

PAWNIE: It's sacrilege – she's too, too marvellous.

    Enter PRESTON *with a tray of cocktails. Everyone helps themselves.*

FLORENCE: What do you think about it, Tom?

TOM: I've never seen her.

FLORENCE: Yes, you have. About three months ago, at the *Comedy*.

TOM: Oh. . . . I don't remember.

PAWNIE: Don't remember! An artist like that! Good God, it's agony!

HELEN: You'll look awfully tired at dinner-time, Pawnie, if you don't calm down a little.

FLORENCE: This is special – my own invention.

HELEN: Absolutely delicious.

TOM: A bit too sweet.

FLORENCE: Tom, *darling*, don't be so taciturn – he's always taciturn after a *matinée*.

PAWNIE: When's Nicky coming back?

FLORENCE: To-morrow, isn't it too divine? He's been away for a whole year, but I saw him for a moment on my way through Paris last month.

PAWNIE: Has he been working hard?

FLORENCE: I suppose so, but you know what Nicky is – bless his heart!

PAWNIE: I heard him play at Yvonne Mirabeau's.

FLORENCE: She's a loathsome woman, isn't she?

HELEN: Not as bad as that.

PAWNIE: She's a half-wit. I can't bear half-wits.

FLORENCE: She goes on so dreadfully about things – devastating.

PAWNIE: Funny Nicky liking her so much.

FLORENCE: Only because she keeps on saying how wonderful he
is – that always appeals to Nicky.

PAWNIE: How old is he now?

FLORENCE: Twenty-four. Isn't it absurd to think I have such a
grown-up son – old General Fenwick said last Thursday
that — (*The telephone rings, she goes to it.*) Hallo – hallo – yes, my
dear, how are you? – Yes, so am I, simply worn out. No,
when? How perfectly marvellous.... No, dear, it's a prescrip-
tion: but I can let you have a little in a jar.... Quite easy, all
you do is just rub it on at night.... Don't be so silly ... not in
the least, if you send the car round that will be all right....
Very well.... Good-bye, darling. (*She hangs up receiver.*) I give
Clara Hibbert ten for stupidity, don't you, Helen?

HELEN: A hundred and ten.

PAWNIE: Ten's the limit.

TOM: I say, Florence – I think I'd better be getting along if I've
got to be dressed and back here by half-past seven —

FLORENCE: You've got half an hour.

TOM: That's not very much.

FLORENCE: The car's outside ... take it and send it straight back.

PAWNIE: Can it drop me, Florence dear? I always feel so much
richer in your car than anyone else's.

FLORENCE: Of course, Pawnie.

   The telephone rings again.

FLORENCE (*at telephone*): Hallo ... yes ... speaking.... How do
you do —?

PAWNIE: Good-bye, Helen, it's been divine —

HELEN: Ring me up at tea-time to-morow.

FLORENCE: ... How perfectly sweet of you ... now, now really
... well, naturally, if you persist in saying such charming
things ... (*laughing gaily*) ... what nonsense....

PAWNIE: Good-bye, Florence —

FLORENCE (*she puts her hand over mouthpiece*): It's that awful

General Fenwick. . . . Good-bye, Pawnie dear, you're coming down to the house on Friday?

PAWNIE: Yes, too lovely —

FLORENCE: Helen's coming by the five o'clock – you'd better travel together.

PAWNIE: Perfect. (*To* TOM.) Are you ready?

TOM: Quite.

PAWNIE (*as they go out*): You *can* drop me first, can't you? I'm not as young as I was —

FLORENCE (*at telephone*): Please forgive me – people rushing in and out, this house grows more like a railway station every day . . . now, General, that was a deliberate compliment. (*She laughs.*) Ridiculous man . . . very well. . . . good-bye. (*She hangs up receiver.*) My God, ten for dreariness!

HELEN: He's not a bad old thing.

FLORENCE: No, but he tries to be, and that's what's so frightful. (*Arranging her hair before glass.*) I look like Death. . . . Isn't Tom a darling?

HELEN: Yes, dear, without being aggressively brilliant.

FLORENCE: I'm afraid, Helen, you're getting rather bitter.

HELEN: Nonsense.

FLORENCE: It's silly to be sarcastic about Tom.

HELEN: It's better than being maudlin about him.

FLORENCE: I don't know what you mean, dear. I'm not in the least maudlin, and never have been about anybody. I sometimes wish I could be – I'm too hard.

HELEN (*taking a cigarette*): Tom will let you down.

FLORENCE: Let me down? Why . . . how . . . I don't understand —

HELEN: You're more in love with him than he is with you.

FLORENCE: Don't be so *absurd*, Helen.

HELEN: It's true.

FLORENCE (*complacently*): He adores me – worships me – he's never seen anyone like me before in his life. I'm something strange . . . exotic —

HELEN: You're more in love with him than he is with you.

FLORENCE: You're getting on my nerves to-day, Helen.

HELEN: You do see that I'm right, don't you?

FLORENCE: If you knew some of the things he's said to me.

HELEN: I can guess them.

FLORENCE: That boy was utterly unawakened until he met me.

HELEN: He's very young.

FLORENCE: I've taught him – everything.

HELEN: Or nothing.

FLORENCE: Helen, I believe you're jealous.

HELEN: Don't be a fool.

FLORENCE: I wish I hadn't this fatal knack of seeing through people.

HELEN: How's David?

FLORENCE: I don't know – he ought to be home soon.

HELEN: Doesn't he ever suspect anything?

FLORENCE: Of course not – he adores me.

HELEN: It seems so strange not to see —

FLORENCE: I'm devoted to David – I'd do anything for him, anything in the world – but he's grown old and I've kept young – it does muddle things up so. I can't help having a temperament, can I?

HELEN: Temperament. . . . No.

FLORENCE: David's always loved me and never understood me – you see, I'm such an extraordinary *mixture*. I have so many *sides* to my character. I adore being at home and running the house and looking after David and Nicky —

HELEN: You don't exactly overdo it.

FLORENCE: Well, Nicky's been away for such ages. Also, one must be in London for the season. You can't expect me to bury myself in the country indefinitely – I shall be there practically all through the spring and summer.

HELEN: Lovely tennis parties and cricket weeks and things —

FLORENCE: Certainly.

HELEN (*kissing her*): You're a divine creature, Florence.

FLORENCE (*basking*): Am I? (*The telephone rings.*) Hallo – yes – speaking. (*To* HELEN *in a whisper.*) It's Inez Zulieta, I never went to her recital. . . . Inez, *darling*, I never recognised your voice . . . didn't you get my note? . . . it was absolutely true, I was in agony. . . . Inez, don't be angry, if you only knew how I longed for the sound of your wonderful, wonderful voice . . .

darling ... Inez, don't be so cruel ... to-morrow, then. (*She hangs up receiver.*) I do wish Inez wasn't so persistent.

HELEN: You never stop encouraging her.

FLORENCE: Oh, Helen, I'm so tired of everyone.

HELEN: Except Tom?

FLORENCE: Yes, except Tom; he's such a darling.

HELEN: How do you think he and Nicky will get on?

FLORENCE: Marvellously – Tom loves music.

HELEN: He says he does.

FLORENCE: My dear, I took him to that Russian thing the other day and he sat entranced from beginning to end.

HELEN: Poor Nicky!

FLORENCE: Why do you say that?

HELEN: Because I sometimes feel it.

FLORENCE (*suddenly furious*): Oh, I wonder why we're such friends – we're so opposite – you don't understand me a bit. I used to think you did, but you've been different lately – unsympathetic.

HELEN: No, I haven't.

FLORENCE: Yes, you have – over Tom – I believe you're in love with him yourself.

HELEN (*smiling*): No – it isn't that.

FLORENCE: Anyhow, you can't bear him being in love with me.

HELEN: I don't think he is – really. I quite realise that he *was* very violently infatuated, but that is wearing off a bit now. I'm beginning to see him as he is. . . .

FLORENCE: No, no, it's not true – you don't understand—

HELEN: We *are* friends, Florence, though we're so 'opposite'. Do you really know the truth – inside you? Or is all this shrill vanity real?

FLORENCE: What's the matter with you?

HELEN: You're ten years older than I am, but when I'm your age I shall be twenty years older than you.

FLORENCE: *Darling*, how deliciously involved – what *can* you mean by that?

HELEN: I mean, I think it's silly not to grow old when the time comes.

She rises and goes towards door.

FLORENCE (*outraged*): Helen! (*There is suddenly heard a violent knocking at the front door.*) What on earth is that?

> *There is a noise outside, then the door bursts open and* NICKY *enters. He is extremely well dressed in travelling clothes. He is tall and pale, with thin, nervous hands.*

FLORENCE: Nicky.

NICKY: Mother.

> *He embraces her.*

FLORENCE: But I'd no idea – I thought you were coming to-morrow.

NICKY: No, to-day – I wrote to you.

FLORENCE: I'm terribly, terribly excited.

NICKY: Helen, dear, how are you?

> *He kisses her.*

HELEN: Splendid, Nicky.

FLORENCE: I can't get over your arriving like this. . . . I never realized —

NICKY: Silly . . . you're looking awfully well.

FLORENCE: Am I?

NICKY: Wonderful, as usual.

FLORENCE: I was talking to George Morrison only last Thursday —

NICKY: The man who wrote that fearful book?

FLORENCE: It isn't a fearful book, it's brilliant – anyhow, he absolutely refused to believe that I had a grown-up son.

HELEN: My dears, I must fly.

NICKY: Don't go yet.

HELEN: I must – I'm hours late as it is.

NICKY: Be a little later, then.

FLORENCE: Remember, five o'clock train on Friday.

NICKY: Oh, is she coming down to the house – divine?

HELEN: Yes, if Florence is still speaking to me – good-bye.

> *She goes out.*

NICKY: Have you been having a scene?

FLORENCE: No, dear.

NICKY: She's a darling – Helen —

FLORENCE: Extremely stupid and tactless sometimes.

NICKY: It doesn't feel as though I'd been away at all.

FLORENCE: I've missed you appallingly – we had such a short time together in Paris – did you enjoy all my letters?

NICKY: I adored them – so did John Bagot. I used to read most of them aloud to him. He's mad on you, saw your pictures in the *Tatler*, or something, and fell in love with it.

FLORENCE: Is he nice?

NICKY: He's grand.

FLORENCE: We must all dine at the Embassy. When is he coming to England?

NICKY: Not until after Christmas.

FLORENCE: You must see my new photographs, they're wonder-ful.

She takes large packet from desk.

NICKY: It's heavenly – being back.

FLORENCE: Look.

NICKY: I don't like that one.

FLORENCE: How can you, Nicky! – Tom likes that one best of all.

NICKY: Who's Tom?

FLORENCE: Tom Veryan – he's a dear, you'll like him frightfully – you know – the very nicest type of Englishman.

NICKY: I hate the very nicest type of Englishman.

FLORENCE: Don't be tiresome, Nicky, he's only twenty-four, and they all think *so* well of him —

NICKY: All who?

FLORENCE: All his officers and people, he's in the Brigade.

NICKY (*holding photograph away from him and scrutinising it through half-closed eyes*): Now that one really is *enchanting* – they've got your hair *beautifully* – Oh, yes, my dear, it's perfect.

FLORENCE (*complacently*): It *is* good – she's sweet – Madame Henderson, she simply won't hear of my paying for these – she says it's quite sufficient to be allowed to exhibit them in the window.

NICKY: Is anyone dining this evening?

FLORENCE: No – Oh, dear, I'd forgotten – I'm dining out with Tom.

NICKY: Oh – I see.

FLORENCE: Your first night home, too – how perfectly fiendish. What a fool I am to have muddled it up.

NICKY: It doesn't matter, darling.

FLORENCE: Oh, but it *does*. I wonder if we could get another seat —

NICKY: Seat, what for?

FLORENCE: We're going to the first night of *The New Elaine*, it's going to be marvellous.

NICKY: Who's in it?

FLORENCE: Nora Dean and Selwyn Steele —

NICKY: Oh, God!

FLORENCE: It's silly of you *always* to jeer at Selwyn Steele. He's a brilliant actor, if only he could get away from his wife. . . .

NICKY: I couldn't bear him to-night, anyway, I'm tired. Is father home yet?

FLORENCE: No, I don't think so. Oh, I do feel such a beast —

NICKY: Don't be silly – honestly, I don't mind a bit.

FLORENCE: I know – you have a nice quiet dinner here and join us at the Embassy afterwards.

NICKY: Is it a late night?

FLORENCE: Yes, they play the most heavenly tune there now – Tom always makes them do it over and over again – I'll put it on —

> *She goes to the gramophone.*

NICKY: How's Iris?

FLORENCE: My dear, don't speak of her.

NICKY: Why – what's she done?

FLORENCE: She's been absolutely foul.

NICKY: In what way?

FLORENCE: Every way – I never trusted her, luckily – Thank God I've got instincts about people – listen, isn't this marvellous – She said the most filthy things to Gloria Craig about me – I always knew she was insanely jealous, but there are limits. I loathe being at people's beck and call. . . . Come and dance.

NICKY (*as they dance*): I'm sorry you've rowed – I rather liked her —

17

FLORENCE: Only because she kept on saying how wonderful you were. . . . She doesn't know a thing about music really.

NICKY: Oh, yes, she does.

FLORENCE: It's merely bluff – all that appreciation – *Darling*, how oddly you're dancing.

NICKY: It's probably because we haven't danced together for so long. . . .

FLORENCE: Anyhow, now she's gone off to Monte Carlo with Violet Fenchurch – silly fool —

Enter DAVID LANCASTER. *He is an elderly grey-haired pleasant man.*

DAVID (*delighted*): Nicky – my boy —

NICKY (*kissing him*): Hallo, father —

DAVID: I thought – Florence said – to-morrow —

NICKY: Mother muddled it up.

DAVID: You look rather tired.

NICKY: I'm splendid – how's everything?

DAVID: The same as usual. I've made lots of improvements down at the house.

FLORENCE: David thinks and talks of nothing but the farm —

DAVID: It's beginning to pay a bit – Peterson's an awfully good man.

NICKY: We'll make a grand tour of it on Sunday.

DAVID: Have you enjoyed yourself in Paris?

NICKY: Oh, yes, rather – it's a splendid place to work.

DAVID: It never struck me that way quite, but still —

FLORENCE: Sophie de Molignac said Nicky's playing had improved wonderfully.

DAVID: I'm so glad, Nicky.

NICKY: I've been doing some Spanish stuff lately.

DAVID: I wish I knew more about it.

NICKY: Never mind, father.

DAVID: Come to my room and talk, I can't bear that thing —

FLORENCE: Father's such a beast, he never will dance with me.

DAVID: Is the *Evening News* anywhere about?

NICKY: Yes, here.

He gives it to him.

DAVID: I'm so glad you're home again, Nicky – don't forget – come and talk. . . .

> *He goes out.*

FLORENCE: David's so much happier in the country.

NICKY: Why on earth doesn't he retire and live at the house for good?

FLORENCE: Work has become such a habit with him – he's always hated giving up habits.

NICKY: Mother – I've got something rather important to tell you.

FLORENCE: Darling, how thrilling! What is it?

NICKY: I am engaged to be married.

FLORENCE: What!

NICKY: Practically – as much as one can be these days.

FLORENCE: Nicky!

NICKY: Don't look so stricken.

FLORENCE: But, Nicky – I never sort of visualised you being engaged, or married, or anything.

NICKY: Why not?

FLORENCE: You're not old enough.

NICKY: I'm twenty-four.

FLORENCE: You don't look it. . . . Thank God!

NICKY: What do you really feel about it, mother?

FLORENCE: *Darling* – I hardly know what to say – you've sprung it on me so suddenly – who is she?

NICKY: A girl called Bunty Mainwaring.

FLORENCE: What a silly name!

NICKY: It isn't at all – it's very attractive.

FLORENCE: Is she an actress, or a student, or what?

NICKY: Neither – she is what is technically termed a 'lady'.

FLORENCE: Do you think she'll like me?

NICKY: She went mad over your photograph.

FLORENCE: Which one?

NICKY: The 'looking out of the window' one.

FLORENCE: That really is one of the best I've ever had done.

NICKY: She said you had the face of an heroic little boy.

FLORENCE: What a *divine* thing to say!

> *She glances at herself in the glass.*

NICKY: She does say divine things – she's supremely intelligent.

FLORENCE: Is she in Paris?

NICKY: No, she came over with me to-day.

FLORENCE: Where does she live?

NICKY: Just round the corner in Carbury Square.

FLORENCE: Near the Churchingtons?

NICKY: It's her mother's house, but her mother's away just now, so I asked her to change quickly and come on here.

FLORENCE: Nicky!

NICKY: Why not? I wanted you to see her as soon as possible.

FLORENCE (*realising parental responsibility*): It's an awful shock, you know.

NICKY: Nonsense, mother – you're quite excited about it, really.

FLORENCE (*with determination*): I shall be charming to her.

NICKY: Then she'll adore you at once – probably too much, and I shall be jealous.

FLORENCE: You'd better both dine here together and come on to the Embassy – how old is she?

NICKY: Twenty-three.

FLORENCE: What does she do?

NICKY: Nothing much – she writes things occasionally.

FLORENCE: Where did you meet her?

NICKY: First of all at a party at Olive Lloyd-Kennedy's.

FLORENCE: I can't bear Olive Lloyd-Kennedy – she's a cat.

NICKY: Then I met her again at Marion Fawcett's – a frightful sort of reception affair – she was staying with her.

FLORENCE: She seems to move exclusively among my worst enemies – is she pretty?

NICKY: I don't know – I haven't really noticed.

FLORENCE (*with a touch of real feeling*): Nicky, darling, I do feel so extraordinary about it.

NICKY: Why extraordinary?

FLORENCE: It's a milestone, isn't it – you being engaged? A definite milestone? (*She catches sight of herself.*) Look at my nose. (*She powders it.*) I do hope she'll like me – I must go and dress now, Tom is fetching me at half-past seven – bring her to my room when she comes.

NICKY: Don't go for a minute.

FLORENCE: I must, really – Tom will be furious.

NICKY: Oh, damn Tom!

FLORENCE: Oh, Nicky, *don't* go and take one of your tiresome prejudices against him.

NICKY (*smiling*): All right, I'll try not to.

FLORENCE: He's frightfully good-looking.

NICKY: Oh!

FLORENCE: And he adores music.

NICKY: Now, then, mother —

FLORENCE: He does, honestly.

NICKY: Good.

FLORENCE: And he dances beautifully.

NICKY: I shall never stop dancing with him.

FLORENCE: And he's so good at games.

NICKY: He sounds adorable.

FLORENCE: Of course, he needs knowing.

NICKY: So do I.

FLORENCE: You will make an effort though, darling, won't you? For my sake?

NICKY: Yes, mother.

FLORENCE: And we'll all have a divine time together, Tom and me and you and what's her name —

NICKY: Bunty.

FLORENCE: Oh, yes, of course, Bunty.

> *Front door bell rings.*

NICKY: This is her, I expect.

FLORENCE: Do you feel wonderful about her?

NICKY: Yes.

FLORENCE: It is thrilling, isn't it – being in love?

NICKY (*frowning a little*): Yes.

FLORENCE: Your father was right – you look awfully tired, Nicky.

NICKY: What nonsense! I feel grand.

> *Enter* PRESTON.

PRESTON (*announcing*): Miss Mainwaring.

> BUNTY *comes in, very self-assured and well dressed. She is more attractive than pretty in a boyish sort of way.*
>
> PRESTON *goes out.*

NICKY: Bunty. You have been quick.

BUNTY: I've simply flown.

NICKY: Bunty ... here is mother....

BUNTY: Oh!

FLORENCE (*taking both her hands*): This is frightfully exciting, isn't it?

> *She kisses her.*

NICKY: I've told her.

BUNTY: Are you furious?

FLORENCE: Of course not – why should I be? 'Specially now.

BUNTY: It's absolutely incredible, you being Nicky's mother.

FLORENCE: Am I anything like you thought I'd be?

BUNTY: Yes, exactly – but I couldn't believe it until I saw you.

FLORENCE: Take off that perfectly divine cloak and have a cigarette – I've got to rush and dress now, because I'm *terribly* late, but you're dining here with Nicky and joining Tom Veryan and me at the Embassy afterwards.

BUNTY: Tom Veryan ... ?

FLORENCE: Yes, do you know him?

BUNTY: I did when I was a child – if it's the same one.

> *She takes off her cloak.*

FLORENCE (*effusively*): Nicky – I don't feel extraordinary about it any more – I'm *delighted*.

NICKY: Angel.

FLORENCE: Perhaps Bunty would like to come down to the house on Friday for the week-end?

NICKY: Oh, yes, marvellous.

BUNTY: It's awfully sweet of you, Mrs Lancaster.

FLORENCE: You must call me Florence – I can't bear Mrs Lancaster. I must fly, Tom will be here at any moment – that's him on the desk.

BUNTY (*going over to photograph*): Yes – it is the same one.

FLORENCE: How too divine ...

> *Telephone rings.*

'Hallo – yes, speaking – Elsa, darling, how are you ... What? ... to-night ... how perfectly heavenly, of course, I'd adore it ... listen, Nicky's just back from Paris, can he come too with

Bunty Mainwaring – yes, he's here. – See you to-night, dear. . . .

Here, Nicky, talk to Elsa. . . .

She snatches up her hand-bag and fur coat and kisses BUNTY *effusively.*

I'm so glad about you and Nicky – it's too wonderful.

She rushes out.

NICKY (*at telephone*): Hallo, Elsa . . . I'd no idea you were in London. I'm terribly thrilled – my dear, you haven't . . . all those lovely tunes you played to me in Paris? . . . *how amazing*, I *am* glad . . . have you done anything with that Tango? . . . You must play it to-night, I want Bunty to hear it. . . . It is perfect, isn't it? . . . Good-bye, dear. (*He hangs up the receiver.*) Bunty.

BUNTY: What?

NICKY: I'm terribly happy.

BUNTY: So am I.

NICKY: Do you remember how we planned all this – coming home together – and breaking it to mother – and everything?

BUNTY: Rather.

NICKY: Do you really like her?

BUNTY: I adore her – she's a perfect angel.

NICKY: I told her your 'heroic little boy' line – she loved it.

BUNTY: It's true, you know – rather defiant too – laughing at Fate.

NICKY: Doesn't Paris seem ages away now?

BUNTY: A different life altogether.

NICKY: That nasty little bit of channel is such an enormous gulf, really. Did you put that dress on on purpose?

BUNTY (*smiling*): Perhaps.

NICKY: You are a devil.

BUNTY: It's such fun being reminded of things.

NICKY: And such agony, too.

BUNTY: Nicky, darling – why agony?

NICKY: It's always agony being in love, and I started loving you in that dress.

BUNTY: Did you?

NICKY: Don't pretend you didn't know.

BUNTY: I suppose one always knows – really.

NICKY: From the very first moment.

BUNTY: Yes.

NICKY: A sort of spark.

BUNTY: Your playing helped a lot.

NICKY: I meant it to.

BUNTY: Calculating pig.

NICKY: Have a cigarette?

BUNTY: All right.

> *He hands her box, and she takes one.*

NICKY (*lighting her cigarette*): I wish we weren't so free.

BUNTY: Why? What do you mean?

NICKY: I feel I should like to elope, or something violently romantic like that.

BUNTY (*laughing*): There wouldn't be much point in it now, would there?

NICKY: Perhaps not. How much do you love me?

BUNTY: I don't know.

NICKY: It's fun analysing one's emotions.

BUNTY: Marvellous fun.

NICKY: And a comfort, too, when things go wrong – but it kills sentiment stone dead.

BUNTY: A good job too.

NICKY: You're frightfully hard, Bunty.

BUNTY: Am I?

NICKY: Much harder than me – really.

BUNTY: You've got so much hysteria.

NICKY: I can't help it.

BUNTY: Of course not, it's your temperament. You burst out suddenly.

NICKY: Not so badly as I used to.

BUNTY: You're growing older.

NICKY: God, yes; isn't it foul?

BUNTY: Hell, my dear.

NICKY: It's funny how mother's generation always longed to be old when they were young, and we strain every nerve to keep young.

BUNTY: That's because we see what's coming so much more clearly.

NICKY: Wouldn't it be terrible to know *exactly* – I feel frightened sometimes.

BUNTY: Why?

NICKY: We're all so hectic and nervy. . . .

BUNTY: It doesn't matter – it probably only means we shan't live so long. . . .

NICKY (*suddenly*): Shut up – shut up. . . .

Enter PRESTON.

PRESTON (*announcing*): Mr Veryan.

Enter TOM. NICKY *greets him and shakes hands. Exit* PRESTON.

NICKY: How are you? – I'm Nicky – I came over to-day instead of to-morrow. . . .

TOM: Oh!

NICKY: Do you know Bunty Mainwaring?

TOM: Bunty – I say – I am glad.

They shake hands warmly.

NICKY: We'd better have some cocktails.

He goes to the door and shouts.

Preston . . . bring us some cocktails. . . .

TOM: This *is* jolly – I didn't know what had become of you.

BUNTY: I've been living in Paris a good deal.

TOM: How many years ago is it since we . . .

BUNTY: During the War – the last time I saw you, you were at Sandhurst.

NICKY: Such a pretty place.

TOM: You've hardly altered a bit – more grown up, of course.

NICKY: All this is most affecting.

TOM: Bunty and I used to know one another awfully well.

NICKY: What fun!

BUNTY (*warningly*): Nicky . . .

NICKY: But it is – it's thrilling – there's nothing so charming as a reunion.

BUNTY: Nicky and I have been travelling all day. . . . Boats and trains get on his nerves. . . .

NICKY: When the cocktails come, tell Preston to bring mine to me in father's room.

BUNTY: Nicky, don't be so silly.

NICKY: Surely it's not silly to want to talk to my aged father after a year's debauch in Paris? I fail to see why you should have the monopoly of reunions.

BUNTY: Well, don't be long.

TOM: Cheerio!

NICKY (crossly): Oh, God!

    He goes out.

TOM: What's up?

BUNTY: These temperamental musicians.

TOM: Silly ass.

BUNTY: He isn't really – he's only jealous.

TOM: Why ... is he ...?

BUNTY: We're by way of being engaged.

TOM: What?

BUNTY: Why not?

TOM: Are you ... are you in love with him?

BUNTY (lightly): Yes – isn't it damnable?

TOM: Good Lord!

    He laughs.

BUNTY: What are you laughing at?

TOM: It seems so funny you being in love with that sort of chap.

BUNTY: What do you mean by 'that sort of chap'?

TOM: Oh – I don't know, that type seems so unlike you.

BUNTY: Type?

TOM: Yes, you know – up in the air – effeminate.

BUNTY: You're more bucolic than you used to be, Tom.

TOM: Here, I say ...

    Enter PRESTON with cocktails.

BUNTY: Will you please take Mr Nicky's in to him in his father's room?

PRESTON: Yes, miss.

TOM: Is Mrs Lancaster nearly ready?

PRESTON: I think so, sir.

TOM: Ask her to hurry – we shall be late.

PRESTON: Yes, sir.

    He goes out.

BUNTY: I can laugh now.

    She does so.

TOM: Why?

BUNTY: I've just realised something.

TOM: What?

BUNTY: We shall meet again – over the week-end.

TOM: Are you coming down to the house?

BUNTY: Yes.

TOM: That's splendid – come for a tramp Sunday morning and we'll talk.

BUNTY: What about?

TOM: Oh, lots of things – old times.

BUNTY (*lifting her cocktail*): Old times, Tom.

TOM (*doing the same*): Cheerio!

CURTAIN

ACT II

The scene is the hall of MRS LANCASTER'S *house, about forty miles from London.*

When the curtain rises it is just after dinner on the Sunday of the week-end party – the gramophone is going, and there is a continual buzz of conversation. CLARA HIBBERT, *an emaciated soprano, is dancing with* TOM VERYAN, HELEN *with* PAWNIE, *and* NICKY *with* BUNTY. FLORENCE *is seated on the club fender talking intellectually with* BRUCE FAIRLIGHT, *an earnest dramatist, the squalor of whose plays is much appreciated by those who live in comparative luxury.*

There must be a feeling of hectic amusement and noise, and the air black with cigarette smoke and superlatives. During the first part of the scene everyone must appear to be talking at once, but the actual lines spoken while dancing must be timed to reach the audience as the speakers pass near the footlights. This scene will probably be exceedingly difficult to produce, but is absolutely indispensable.

HELEN: It's much too fast, Nicky.

TOM: Do slow down a bit.

NICKY: It's the place that's marked on the record.

PAWNIE: I've never danced well since the War, I don't know why.

FLORENCE: But your last act was so strong, when she came in half mad with fright and described everything minutely.

BRUCE: I try to write as *honestly* as possible.

CLARA: I gave her three for manners, but seven for charm, because I had to be a *little* nice!

TOM: I thought she was rather a decent sort.

BUNTY: No, but really, Nicky, his technique completely annihilated his inspiration.

NICKY: Not with Debussy and Ravel, with the older Masters, yes; but he's probably tired of them.

BUNTY: That's so stupid, I think.

HELEN: My dear, it was the most 'Chic' thing you've ever seen, but unfortunately the wrong colour.

PAWNIE: Marion Ferris had that Poiret model copied in the most frightful blue!

CLARA: I believe my shoe's coming off.

TOM: Shall we stop?

CLARA: No, it's all right.

FLORENCE: I wonder if you could gouge this cigarette-end out of the holder for me?

BRUCE: I'll try (*He does so.*) I always smoke a pipe when I'm working.

FLORENCE: How soothing!

BUNTY: I suppose one can never really judge properly from a recital.

NICKY: Not with him, because he's not dramatic enough.

BUNTY: Dramatic pianists make me uncomfortable.

HELEN: Pawnie, your tongue grows more venomous every day.

PAWNIE (*giggling*): Well, I had to say something – anyhow, it was true.

HELEN: Especially about her ankles.

PAWNIE: My dear, yes!

> *They both laugh.*
> *The record comes to an end, and* NICKY *begins to change it.*
> *Everyone talks and laughs.*

CLARA: You must come next Sunday week.

TOM: Thanks awfully, I'd love to.

CLARA: I'm only singing ballads, but you know what Sunday concerts are.

TOM: Oh, yes, rather.

CLARA (*to* NICKY): What's on the other side?

NICKY: 'You've got the cutest ears and eyes and nose'.

PAWNIE: Do put on 'Spoony Moon in Upper Carolina'.

HELEN: No, don't put it on, Nicky, play it yourself; you always make a gramophone go too quickly.

BUNTY: Yes, go on, Nicky.

FLORENCE (*refusing* BRUCE'S *offer of a cigarette*): No, thanks, not another – I'm dancing with Tom.

BUNTY (*gaily*): Missing one, Tom.

TOM: Righto!

> NICKY *commences to play a foxtrot.*

BUNTY (*dragging* BRUCE *to his feet*): Come on, Mr Fairlight, don't overdo the serious dramatist stunt!

BRUCE: I warn you I'm no good.

> *He dances with her, and confirms the truth of his warning.* CLARA HIBBERT *squashes down on the piano-seat next to* NICKY *and endeavours with one finger in the treble to follow the tune he is playing.* HELEN *and* PAWNIE *stand right down close to the footlights, smoking and talking, their backs are half-turned to the audience, but their remarks must be perfectly audible.*

HELEN: Tom Veryan doesn't dance as well as he thinks he does.

PAWNIE: With that figure he ought to be marvellous.

HELEN: He's too athletic.

PAWNIE: Anyhow, I'm sure he's a success at the Bath Club.

HELEN: Doesn't Florence look astounding?

PAWNIE: Absolutely. She knows exactly what suits her.

HELEN: Where's David?

PAWNIE: He went off to his study to smoke.

HELEN: I do wish Florence wouldn't be irritable with him in front of everybody. I felt acutely uncomfortable at dinner.

PAWNIE: It makes Nicky furious as a rule, but to-night he was too occupied with that stupid little fool Bunty Mainwaring to take any notice.

HELEN: She's an excellent type.

PAWNIE: Very average; I only hope nothing will come of Nicky's mania for her.

HELEN: I don't think we need worry.

PAWNIE: Why?

HELEN: Wait and see, my dear.

CLARA (*leaving* NICKY *at the piano and advancing on* PAWNIE): Come and dance, Pawnie, and tell me how divinely I sang on Tuesday.

PAWNIE (*agreeably*): You didn't.

CLARA: Ten for cruelty.

They start to dance. HELEN *moves over to the mantelpiece for a cigarette.*

HELEN: Have you a match, Nicky?

NICKY: Isn't this a marvellous tune?

HELEN: Fascinating! (*She goes over and sits next to him. Gently slipping her hand into his coat pocket.*) Darling, I *do* want a match. (*She brings out a little box.*) What a divine little box!

NICKY *stops playing and jumps up.*

NICKY (*violently*): Helen, give that to me —

Everyone stops dancing.

CLARA: Nicky, dear, *don't* be tiresome.

NICKY (*recovering himself*): I'm sick of playing, let's have the gramophone again. (*To* HELEN.) Here's a light, dearie.

He takes match-box out of another pocket and lights HELEN'S *cigarette. She looks at him queerly for a moment, then he restarts the gramophone and everyone begins to dance again except* HELEN *and* BRUCE FAIRLIGHT. HELEN *goes over to the fireplace and takes a coffee-cup from the mantelpiece.*

HELEN: Whose coffee is this? Someone drank mine, and I'd hardly touched it.

BRUCE: If it has no sugar in it, it's mine.

HELEN (*draining it*): It had no sugar in it.

FLORENCE: You're dancing abominably, Tom.

TOM: Oh, am I?

FLORENCE: What's the matter with you?

TOM: I don't know, I suppose I'm tired.

FLORENCE: You're not usually tired when you're dancing with me.

TOM: Oh, Florence, don't nag!

FLORENCE: How dare you speak to me like that?

She stops dancing and goes over to the fireplace.

TOM (*following her*): I say, Florence – I'm sorry —

PAWNIE: Let's stop the music for a moment and think of something really marvellous to do.

BUNTY: No, let's go on dancing.

CLARA: I'm exhausted.

PAWNIE (*stopping the gramophone*): What was that divine game we played coming back from Paris, Helen?

HELEN: Just ordinary 'Clumps', wasn't it?

BUNTY: I loathe 'Clumps'.

NICKY: What about the History game?

BRUCE: What's that?

BUNTY: Oh, no, Nicky, it's too intellectual.

FLORENCE: There's a Mah-jong set in the drawing-room.

PAWNIE: How divine – let's make up a table immediately.

CLARA: I won't be happy until someone gives me a set made entirely of jade.

NICKY: Come on, Bunty.

BUNTY (*looking at* TOM): I can't play it.

NICKY: You can; you used to play it in Paris with Yvonne.

BUNTY: I've forgotten it.

NICKY: You'll soon remember again.

> *He drags her off.*

PAWNIE: Come along, Clara.

CLARA: I insist on Mr Fairlight learning.

BRUCE: I'm afraid I'm no good at that sort of thing.

CLARA: You'll be able to put it in one of your plays.

PAWNIE: Come and watch, it's too thrilling for words.

> CLARA, BRUCE *and* PAWNIE *go off.*

HELEN: Have you only one set, Florence?

FLORENCE: Yes, isn't it maddening? Clara promised to bring hers down but forgot.

HELEN: Does Bruce Fairlight play Bridge?

FLORENCE: No, I don't think so.

HELEN: Dramatists are such a comfort in a house-party, aren't they?

> *She goes off.*

TOM: Aren't you coming, Florence?

FLORENCE: No.

TOM (*nonplussed*): Oh!

FLORENCE: But please don't let me stop *you* going, I'm sure you're *dying* to be with the others.

TOM: I say, Florence, I wish you wouldn't go on like that.

FLORENCE: I don't know what is the matter with you, you've never behaved like this before.

TOM: I haven't behaved like anything.

FLORENCE: You've been exceedingly rude to me, both at dinner and afterwards.

TOM: I wasn't at dinner.

FLORENCE: Yes, you were; you snapped me up when I said I didn't like Elsie Saunders.

TOM: You know perfectly well she's a friend of mine.

FLORENCE: Well, she oughtn't to be, after the things she's said about me.

TOM: You will go on imagining.

FLORENCE: Nothing of the sort – I *know!* If you weren't so dense you'd see, too – the jealousy I have to put up with. I get so tired of it all, so desperately tired.

> *She becomes a little pathetic.*

TOM: Talk about being different, you're different too —

FLORENCE: I'm unhappy.

TOM: Why?

FLORENCE: Because I hate to see you being put against me.

TOM: Florence!

FLORENCE: You'll understand one day. They're all very subtle, but I can see.

TOM: Nobody's said a word to me about you, they'd better not try.

FLORENCE: Why, what would you do?

TOM: I'd – I'd be furious.

FLORENCE: Oh!

TOM: And I'd let them see it, too.

FLORENCE (*holding out her hands*): Tom —

TOM: Yes?

FLORENCE: I forgive you.

TOM: I can't bear you being angry with me.

FLORENCE: Can't you, really?

TOM: It makes me feel beastly.

FLORENCE: Come and sit here.

TOM (*sitting next to her on the club fender*): That's a lovely dress.

FLORENCE: It is sweet, isn't it?

TOM: You always wear wonderful clothes.

FLORENCE: Do I, Tom?

TOM: You know you do.

FLORENCE: Do you remember the very first time we met?

TOM: Rather.

FLORENCE: Oxford's so full of romance, isn't it?

TOM: It was when you came down.

FLORENCE: Thank you, Tom, dear.

TOM: We did have fun.

FLORENCE: You used to come up to *matinées*, and I'd motor you back afterwards.

TOM: Ripping!

FLORENCE: That reminds me, I've got seats for *Rolling Stones* on Tuesday – don't forget.

TOM: You never said you were going to get them.

FLORENCE: It doesn't matter, I thought I did. We'd better dine at Claridges.

TOM: But, Florence, I – I can't come!

FLORENCE: Why not?

TOM: I promised to go out.

FLORENCE: Who with?

TOM: Mother.

FLORENCE: Can't you put her off, it will be such a good first night?

TOM: Well – you see, as a matter of fact – it's rather awkward – I put her off the other day —

There is a slight pause.

FLORENCE (*a trifle coldly*): Oh, well, never mind, we'll go some other night.

Enter DAVID.

DAVID: Hallo, Florence, I thought you were in the drawing-room.

FLORENCE: They're playing Mah-jong, and there's only one set. I shall break in presently.

TOM: I'll just go and see how they're getting on.

This obvious excuse for getting out of the room is not lost upon FLORENCE.

34

FLORENCE: Yes, do.

TOM: Come and play soon.

He goes out quietly.

FLORENCE: Don't you think this is a divine frock?

DAVID: Very pretty.

FLORENCE: You and Helen seemed to be very thick at dinner. What were you talking about?

DAVID: Nothing much – I like Helen.

FLORENCE: Only because she flatters you and listens to everything you say.

DAVID: She doesn't flatter me.

FLORENCE: I suppose she was talking about the farm, and giving her opinions.

DAVID: We did discuss the farm a little.

FLORENCE: She doesn't know a thing about it, really.

DAVID: Perhaps not, but it passed the time.

He goes out.

FLORENCE sits still for a moment, then she wearily buries her face in her hands. Enter NICKY.

NICKY (*going to her*): What's the matter, darling?

FLORENCE: Nothing, I've got a slight headache.

NICKY: Why don't you go Byes?

FLORENCE: I can't, it's much too early.

NICKY: I'm sick of Mah-jong.

FLORENCE: Who's playing now?

NICKY: Pawnie and Helen and Clara are trying to teach Bruce Fairlight, he's an awful fool at it.

He sits down at the piano and plays absently.

FLORENCE: You must get Bunty out of that habit of contradicting everything people say.

NICKY: I don't see why.

FLORENCE: It's bad breeding.

NICKY (*striking a note viciously*): Who cares nowadays? We've all got a right to our opinions.

FLORENCE: She seems to forget that I'm much older than she is.

NICKY: That's no argument, mother; it's silly only to remember your age when someone says something you don't like.

35

FLORENCE: She's having a bad effect on you.

NICKY: Nonsense!

FLORENCE: You've changed since Paris.

NICKY: Naturally.

FLORENCE: You never used to be rude to me.

NICKY: Oh, damn, I'm not rude.

FLORENCE: Yes, you are.

NICKY: Well, don't start running down Bunty.

FLORENCE: Stop playing – stop playing!

NICKY (getting up angrily): Oh, God!

He goes towards door and collides with HELEN.

HELEN: What's happening?

FLORENCE: Nothing, Bunty's just putting Nicky against me. I knew she'd try to.

She goes out.

HELEN: You must be having a delightful evening! You leave the drawing-room having rowed with Bunty, and come here and row with Florence.

NICKY: Mother's impossible.

HELEN: She's no different from what she's always been.

NICKY: Well, I haven't realised it before.

HELEN (taking a cigarette and lighting it): You haven't been engaged before.

NICKY: I'm hating this house-party.

HELEN (lightly): Don't say that, dear, it's not kind.

NICKY: You know I don't mean you.

HELEN: Are you very much in love?

NICKY: Yes. – No. – I don't know.

HELEN: I wonder.

NICKY: It's utterly devastating, anyhow.

HELEN: When did you meet her?

NICKY: About five months ago.

HELEN: What was she doing in Paris?

NICKY: Oh, I don't know – fooling about.

HELEN: Splendid.

NICKY: She's been studying French literature.

HELEN: Why?

NICKY: She's going to write – herself – some day.

HELEN: Oh, I see!

NICKY: Helen, do you like her?

HELEN: I can't tell yet – yesterday was the first time I'd ever set eyes on her.

NICKY: She's wonderfully intelligent.

HELEN: Yes – I'm sure she is.

NICKY: You *don't* like her?

HELEN: I tell you – I'm not sure yet.

NICKY: It's generally the way – one's friends always hate one another.

HELEN (*smiling*): It *is* difficult for you, isn't it?

NICKY: I should so like you to like her.

HELEN: Very well – I'll try.

NICKY: She's utterly opposite to me in every way.

HELEN: Yes, I see that.

NICKY: But that's as it ought to be, isn't it?

HELEN: It depends.

NICKY: I need a sort of restraining influence terribly.

HELEN: Yes, Nicky.

NICKY: She's awfully good for me.

HELEN: Is she?

NICKY: Yes – she curbs me when I get temperamental and silly.

HELEN: I always felt you needed encouraging more than curbing.

NICKY (*laughing*): Oh, Helen – aren't you a darling!

HELEN: I mean it.

NICKY: You're wrong, though – I'm all over the place.

HELEN: Anyhow, I do hope you'll be very happy with her.

NICKY: I don't suppose I shall ever be that – I haven't got the knack.

HELEN: Do you work hard?

NICKY: Yes.

HELEN: Really hard?

NICKY: Frightfully.

HELEN: Liar!

NICKY: If you'd seen me in Paris – studying, studying – all night long until the grey dawn put the guttering candle to shame – and my nerveless hands dropped from the keys —

HELEN: Candles gutter awfully quickly when they're burnt at both ends.

NICKY: Meaning that I look a debauched wreck of my former self?

HELEN: Exactly.

NICKY: If you go on encouraging me at this rate I shall commit suicide.

HELEN: You do resent anyone taking a real interest in you, don't you?

NICKY: I distrust it.

HELEN: Why?

NICKY: I don't know – I'm not worth it.

HELEN: You seem to be suffering from a slight inferiority complex.

NICKY: Not a bit of it – I'm gay and witty and handsome.

HELEN: Oh, Nicky, you're so maddening.

NICKY: Don't be cross, Helen.

HELEN: I'm one of the few people who know what you're really like, and you won't give me the credit for it.

NICKY: Do you think you do, honestly?

HELEN: Yes – and I'm exceedingly worried about you.

NICKY: You needn't be.

HELEN: You're sensitive and reserved and utterly foolish.

NICKY: Thank you – I'm beginning to feel beautifully picturesque.

HELEN: And you're scared.

NICKY: Why! What have I to be scared about?

HELEN: Would you like me to tell you?

NICKY: No.

HELEN: Why not?

NICKY: Because you're a sentimentalist, and you see things that aren't there at all.

HELEN: You're far more sentimental than I.

NICKY: Darling Helen – you've got such a lovely mind – like a Christmas card – with frosted robins and sheep wandering about in the snow – bleating.

HELEN: All the same, I should give up drugs if I were you.

NICKY: Helen!

HELEN: Well?

NICKY: I don't know what you mean.

HELEN: Do you think I can't see?

NICKY (*forcing a laugh*): You're being terribly funny, aren't you?

HELEN: You fool! You unutterable little fool!

NICKY: Don't be dramatic, dear.

HELEN: I thought you had common sense; I credited you with more intelligence than that.

NICKY: If you persist in being absurd.

HELEN (*suddenly with intense feeling*): Nicky, don't resist me, don't fight me, I'm your friend, I wouldn't have said a word if I weren't. You've got to stop it; you haven't gone very far yet, there's still time – for God's sake listen to reason.

NICKY: Shut up, shut up, don't speak so loudly.

HELEN: Nicky, throw it away.

NICKY: When did you find out?

HELEN: To-night, you know, when you were playing, but I've guessed for ages.

NICKY: You needn't be frightened, Helen, I only take just the tiniest little bit, once in a blue moon!

HELEN: If anything goes wrong, you'll take a lot – throw it away.

NICKY: What could go wrong?

HELEN: Never mind, throw it away!

NICKY: I can't – look out, somebody's coming.

> *Enter* DAVID.

DAVID: Hallo!

NICKY: Hallo, father!

DAVID: What's the matter?

NICKY: The matter – why?

DAVID: You look very worried.

NICKY: Helen and I have just had a grand heart-to-heart talk; we've undone our back hair, loosened our stays and wallowed in it.

DAVID: Oh, I see!

HELEN: We haven't seen one another for so long – it was inevitable.

DAVID: You never came and looked at the Farm this morning – I waited for you.

NICKY: I'm awfully sorry, father – I just went on sleeping.

HELEN: I'll see you later, Nicky.

NICKY: All right.

HELEN *goes out.*

DAVID: How do you think your mother's looking?

NICKY: Splendid – the same as ever.

DAVID: Would you like a cigar?

NICKY: No thanks, father – I'm not very good at them.

DAVID: I was just on my way to bed – there are far too many people in the house.

NICKY (*smiling*): You must be used to that by now.

DAVID: You ought to stay down here, you know – during the week and get some fresh air.

NICKY: I've got such millions of things to do in London.

DAVID: Worth doing?

NICKY: Yes, of course.

DAVID: You look as though you needed a rest.

NICKY: You needn't worry about me – I feel splendid.

DAVID: She seems a nice girl.

NICKY: Who – Bunty?

DAVID: Yes. Quiet and untiresome.

NICKY: She's a darling!

DAVID: When do you propose to get married?

NICKY: I don't know – the engagement's only a sort of try-out, you know.

DAVID: Oh, I see – I didn't realise that – I'm so unversed in modern technicalities.

NICKY: It's her idea really – just to tread water for a bit.

DAVID: It sounds an excellent plan.

NICKY: I'm awfully glad you like her.

DAVID: Is she musical?

NICKY: Oh, yes – frightfully!

DAVID: Good!

NICKY: Father, I think I will come down here for a few days – and work quietly.

DAVID: If you do that I'll only go up to London every other day – I see so little of you when you're at the flat.

NICKY: That's settled then. I wonder what mother will say!

DAVID: I'll talk to her.

NICKY: All right – she won't bother about us much.

DAVID: No – I don't suppose she will – I think I'll be getting along to bed now. Good night, my boy!

NICKY: Good night, father!

> *They shake hands, and* DAVID *pats* NICKY'S *shoulder rather tentatively. He goes upstairs and* NICKY *wanders to the piano. He plays absently, and* BUNTY *enters.*

BUNTY: I want to talk to you.

NICKY (*still playing*): All right.

BUNTY: Perhaps you'd stop playing for a minute.

NICKY: Won't you let me woo you with a little Scriabin?

BUNTY: Please stop.

NICKY (*rising*): I'm unappreciated – that's what it is.

> *There is a slight pause – he goes over to her.*

I say, Bunty —

BUNTY: What?

NICKY: Before you say anything awful to me, I *am* sorry for being rude just now.

BUNTY: So you ought to be.

NICKY: Will you forgive me?

BUNTY: Yes, I forgive you.

NICKY: I've been irritable all the evening.

BUNTY: Give me a cigarette, Nicky.

NICKY: Here.

> *They both smoke.*

BUNTY: Thanks.

NICKY: What did you want to talk to me about?

BUNTY: Lots of things – Us!

NICKY (*hardening*): Oh, I see!

BUNTY: Don't you think it's rather silly – being engaged?

NICKY: No, not at all.

BUNTY: I do.

NICKY: Just because we bickered a bit to-night?

BUNTY: No, not only because of that.

NICKY: Why then?

BUNTY: Can't you see?

41

NICKY: No.

BUNTY: Well, we're not very suited to one another are we?

NICKY: Why do you suddenly say that?

BUNTY: Because I've only just realised it.

NICKY: I'm sorry.

BUNTY: It's not your fault particularly.

NICKY: I'm glad.

BUNTY: It's circumstances and surroundings.

NICKY: Oh, that can be altered quite easily. We'll change the shape of the house – we'll take all that wall away and turn that into a studio – you love studios, don't you? – then we'll transform the drawing-room into an enormous aviary.

BUNTY: It's practically that now!

NICKY: And then we'll —

BUNTY: Shut up, Nicky!

NICKY: I'm only trying to be amenable.

BUNTY: Are you, really?

NICKY: Yes, I'm putting up a sort of defence, Bunty. I have a feeling that you're going to be unpleasant, and I want to establish myself comfortably before you start.

BUNTY: I don't want to be unpleasant – only honest.

NICKY: You won't let the two run together, will you?

BUNTY (*with vehemence*): You're hopeless, hopeless, hopeless!

NICKY: Yes – I think I am rather.

BUNTY: In a way I'm glad – it makes it easier.

NICKY: Does it?

BUNTY: You're not in love with me, really – you couldn't be!

NICKY: Please, don't say that.

BUNTY: Why don't you face things properly?

NICKY: One generally has to in the end – I like to put it off for as long as possible.

BUNTY: That's cowardly.

NICKY: Don't be pompous, darling.

BUNTY: You're a great help, I must say.

NICKY: Why should I help to destroy my own happiness?

BUNTY: That's self-pity and self-deception.

NICKY: Why are you going on like this?

BUNTY: Because I tell you – I've realised the truth.

NICKY: I suppose you've taken a hatred to mother!

BUNTY: No, not a hatred.

NICKY: You don't like her.

BUNTY: Not very much.

NICKY: Why not? She likes you.

BUNTY: She detests me.

NICKY: Nonsense, why should she?

BUNTY: Because I'm young.

NICKY: What a filthy thing to say!

BUNTY: It's true.

NICKY: It's nothing of the sort.

BUNTY: You're so stupid sometimes.

NICKY: Thank you.

BUNTY: Don't let's start bickering again.

NICKY: We won't discuss mother any more then.

BUNTY: You started it.

NICKY: I wish I could make you understand her like I do – I mean she's awfully irritating, I know – but deep down she's marvellous in spite of everything.

BUNTY (*coldly*): Everything?

NICKY (*vehemently*): Yes, *everything!* Don't be a beast, Bunty, just try to see her point a little, even if you do dislike her. She is terribly silly about being 'young', I know, but she's been used to so much admiration and flattery and everything always, she feels she sort of can't give it up – you do see that, don't you? And she hasn't really anything in the least comforting to fall back upon, she's not clever – real kind of brain cleverness – and father's no good, and I'm no good, and all the time she's wanting life to be as it was instead of as it is. There's no harm in her anywhere – she's just young inside. Can't you imagine the utter foulness of growing old? 'Specially if you've been lovely and attractive like she was. The beautiful Flo Lancaster! She used to be known as that – I can remember her when I was quite small, coming up to say good night to me, looking too perfectly radiant for words – and she used to come to the school, too, sometimes, and everyone used to go mad over her, and I used to get frightfully proud and excited —

BUNTY: I've never heard you talk like this before.

NICKY: I don't think I ever have.

BUNTY: I like you better clear cut, not blurred by sentiment.

> NICKY *looks at her for a moment in amazement.*

NICKY: To describe you as hard would be inadequate – you're metallic!

BUNTY: I can see straight.

NICKY (*politely*): Can you?

BUNTY: Yes. We could never be happy together.

NICKY: Perhaps not.

BUNTY: Shall we just – finish – then?

NICKY: Certainly, I'm sorry we were too modern to have an engagement ring, you'd have been able to give it back to me so beautifully.

BUNTY: Don't be ridiculous!

NICKY: Better than being blurred by sentiment.

> BUNTY *lights another cigarette and, kicking off her shoes, perches on the club fender and proceeds to warm her feet at the fire.*
>
> *Enter* CLARA HIBBERT.

CLARA: My dear, I'm *shattered* – and I'm going straight to bed – probably for several weeks.

BUNTY: Why?

CLARA: Shshsh! He's coming.

BUNTY: Who's coming!

CLARA: Bruce Fairlight – I've been teaching him Mah-jong – these master brains – agony, dear —

> *Enter* BRUCE FAIRLIGHT.

BRUCE: Very interesting, that game.

CLARA (*weakly*): I thought you'd like it.

BRUCE: It's interesting *psychologically!* The concentration and suspense —

> *Enter* FLORENCE, HELEN, PAWNIE *and* TOM. TOM *is grasping a whisky and soda –* PAWNIE *is eating a biscuit.*

PAWNIE: I'm quite exhausted – it must be the country air —

FLORENCE: – it was too lovely, because I started with two red dragons in my hand —

HELEN: I wondered who had them —

PAWNIE: One more tune, Nicky, before we go to bed —

FLORENCE: Yes, just one —

NICKY (*looking at* BUNTY): I'll play 'I love you!' – such a romantic tune.

> *He puts on the gramophone.*

BUNTY: Do.

HELEN: What time's everyone going up in the morning?

FLORENCE: The ten o'clock's the best – we'll have breakfast at nine downstairs.

PAWNIE (*confidentially*): Do you know that in London I can never do more than nibble a piece of thin toast, and whenever I'm away I eat *enormously!*

NICKY: How very peculiar!

PAWNIE: Your tone revolts me, Nicky – you must never be irascible with your old friends.

NICKY: I haven't got any.

HELEN: Nicky!

NICKY: Sorry, Helen.

FLORENCE: I don't know what's the matter with Nicky – he's been in a vile temper all the evening – his first week-end home, too.

NICKY: Such a pity, when so much trouble has been taken to make me happy and cosy.

TOM: Come and dance, Bunty.

BUNTY: No, not now.

NICKY: Dance with him, Bunty – chaps must have exercise.

FLORENCE: You dance with Bunty, Pawnie – I'll dance with Tom – come on.

> *She and* TOM *dance.*

HELEN: The great thing in this world is not to be obvious, Nicky – over *anything!*

> FLORENCE *and* TOM *dance, also* HELEN *and* PAWNIE. *Everyone talks at once, as in the beginning of the act.*

PAWNIE: You are infuriating, Helen – it's a wonderful book.

HELEN: Thoroughly second-rate.

PAWNIE: What do you think about *Mischievous Passion*, Fairlight?

BRUCE: I never read novels on principle.

PAWNIE: Well, you must read this – it's colossal.

HELEN: Don't be led away by Pawnie, Mr Fairlight, he has no discrimination.

PAWNIE: But I tell you it's brilliant! Absolutely *brilliant!*

HELEN: Nonsense.

PAWNIE: There are times, Helen, when I could willingly see you dead at my feet.

FLORENCE: A little slower, for Heaven's sake!

NICKY: How's that?

> *He makes it far too slow.*

FLORENCE: I think you'd better go to bed, Nicky.

HELEN: We're all going, anyhow.

NICKY: Not yet, please, mummy dear – I'm having such a lovely time!

> *He slams off in a rage.*

PAWNIE: I always knew the Continent was fatal for the young.

BUNTY: Nicky's upset – it's my fault – we're not engaged any more.

FLORENCE: Why – what's happened?

BUNTY: Nothing happened – it was never very serious, really.

HELEN: I had a feeling that it was.

BUNTY: You were wrong.

FLORENCE: Well, I must say it's all been rather abrupt.

BUNTY: It's better to finish things off at once – cleanly – if you're not quite sure, don't you think?

FLORENCE: Well, I'm sorry, Bunty – if you feel like that about it there's nothing more to be said.

BUNTY: I wouldn't have mentioned it at all – only you all seemed to be blaming him for being irritable —

HELEN: Poor Nicky!

CLARA: I really must go up to bed now. I'm so tired. Good night, Florence dear.

FLORENCE: Good night, Clara. Breakfast at nine. Have you got books and everything you want?

CLARA: Yes, thanks. Good night, everyone.

> *Everyone murmurs good night politely.*

FLORENCE: Tom, be an angel and fetch me a glass of milk – it's in the drawing-room.

TOM: All right.

He goes off.

HELEN: Come on up, Florence, I'm dead.

FLORENCE: So am I. Will you turn out the lights when you come?

PAWNIE: With beautiful precision, dear.

FLORENCE (*as she and* HELEN *go upstairs*): Tell Tom to bring my milk up to me, somebody.

PAWNIE: All right.

FLORENCE: Good night, Mr Fairlight.

BRUCE: Good night.

PAWNIE: Good night, Florence.

FLORENCE *and* HELEN *go off.*

BRUCE: I suppose we'd all better go up.

BUNTY: I don't feel I could sleep yet.

Re-enter TOM *with a glass of milk.*

TOM: Hallo! where's Florence!

BUNTY: Gone up to bed – will you take her milk to her?

PAWNIE: What's become of Nicky?

TOM: In the smoking-room, I think.

BRUCE: Good night, Miss Mainwaring.

BUNTY: Good night.

They shake hands.

PAWNIE: I shall come, too – good night.

TOM: Good night.

PAWNIE (*to* BRUCE *as they go upstairs*): When you're writing, do your characters grow as you go along?

BRUCE: No, I think each one out minutely beforehand.

PAWNIE: How too intriguing!

They go off.

TOM: So you've broken it off already?

BUNTY: Yes.

TOM: I didn't know you were going to do it so soon.

BUNTY: It's better to get things over.

TOM: What did he say?

BUNTY: Nothing much.

TOM: Was he furious?

BUNTY: Oh! what does it matter? Don't let's go on about it.

TOM: It's all damned awkward.

BUNTY: What?

TOM: The whole thing.

BUNTY: You're rather scared, aren't you?

TOM: No, not exactly – now that I've got you to back me up.

BUNTY: I shall be glad when we're out of this house.

TOM: So shall I.

BUNTY: I hate the atmosphere.

TOM: I don't know how I've stood it for so long.

BUNTY: You didn't notice it until I came, any more than I noticed
Nicky's atmosphere until you came.

TOM: It's queer, isn't it?

BUNTY: We're reverting to type, don't you see?

TOM: How d'you mean?

BUNTY: Never mind, it's true.

TOM: Do you think I'm being a cad to Florence?

BUNTY: Yes, I do rather.

TOM: But, Bunty! You said this morning —

BUNTY: That I didn't see how you could help yourself, neither I
do – it's frightfully difficult, but it's not altogether your fault,
any more than it would have been mine if I'd married Nicky.
One gets carried away by glamour, and personality, and
magnetism – they're beastly treacherous things.

TOM: You are wonderful.

BUNTY: Don't be silly.

TOM: You're so cool and clear, and you see everything.

BUNTY: I'm sorry – for Nicky.

TOM: Oh, damn Nicky!

BUNTY (laughing): Oh, Tom!

TOM: Why, what's up?

BUNTY: You're so dead set.

TOM: You're worth ten of him any day. What's the use of a chap
like that? He *doesn't do* anything except play the piano – he
can't play any games, he's always trying to be funny —

BUNTY: Shut up, Tom, you're being rather cheap; I haven't reverted to type so quickly that I can't see some of the things I'm missing.

TOM: I wish I knew what you were talking about.

BUNTY: Oh, God! I feel so miserable!

She bursts into tears.

TOM (*flummoxed*): I say – Bunty – for Heaven's sake —

He puts his arms round her.

BUNTY (*shaking him off*): Don't, don't – give me my shoes —

He picks up her shoes; she puts them on. She is half sobbing all the time.

TOM: I say, old girl, hadn't you better go to bed? You're all wrought up!

BUNTY: He said beastly things.

TOM: I'll wring his neck.

BUNTY (*with a fresh burst of tears*): Shut up, Tom, shut up —

TOM: Bunty, stop crying – there's a dear – please, please stop crying —

He takes her in his arms and kisses her, she is groping for her handkerchief. FLORENCE *comes quietly downstairs.*

BUNTY: I can't find my hanky!

TOM: Here's mine.

FLORENCE (*like a pistol shot*): Tom!

TOM *and* BUNTY *break away.*

TOM: Yes, Florence?

FLORENCE (*ominously*): What does this mean?

TOM: I'm sorry, Florence – I —

FLORENCE: You utter cad!

BUNTY: Look here – I should like to say —

FLORENCE: Be quiet – mind your own business.

NICKY *enters.*

NICKY (*seeing tears on* BUNTY'S *face*): What's the matter – is anybody hurt?

FLORENCE (*ominously*): No, not hurt!

BUNTY: I banged my hand, that's all.

FLORENCE: Liar!

NICKY: Mother – don't be so stupid —

TOM: Florence – I —

FLORENCE: Don't *speak* to me —

NICKY (*quietly*): Mother – not now – not now – it's all wrong – control yourself! Bunty – Bunty – do go to bed – please.

He goes to the piano and begins to play jazz.

BUNTY: All right – Tom —

FLORENCE goes to the fireplace, trembling with rage. NICKY *goes on playing.* TOM *and* BUNTY *go towards the stairs.*

FLORENCE: Stop – I want an explanation, please!

BUNTY: How dare you speak to me like that?

FLORENCE: Get out of my house! Get out of my house!

BUNTY: This is disgusting!

TOM: I say, Florence —

FLORENCE: Get out of my house!

BUNTY: I shall leave the first thing in the morning, it's much too late to-night.

She goes off.

NICKY *never stops playing for a moment.*

FLORENCE: Tom. (*He goes towards her absolutely silent.*) You kissed her – you kissed her – I saw you —!

TOM: Yes.

FLORENCE: In this house!

TOM: Yes, Florence, I apologise.

FLORENCE: Apologise! You're beneath contempt – never speak to me again, never touch me again – I hate you!

TOM: Look here, Florence – I'm desperately sorry – you see, I'm afraid I love her.

FLORENCE (*hysterically*): You dare to stand there and say that to me? It's incredible – after all I've done for you – after all we've been to one another. Love! You don't know what it means. You've lied to me – all these months. It's contemptible – humiliating. Get out of my sight!

TOM (*turning and going upstairs*): Very well.

FLORENCE (*suddenly realising that he is gone*): Tom – Tom – come back – come back —!

She runs upstairs after him. NICKY *at last stops playing and lets his hands drop from the keys.*

CURTAIN

ACT III

The scene is FLORENCE'S *bedroom the same night – about two hours have elapsed. When the curtain rises* FLORENCE *is lying face downwards on the bed, she is dressed in a very beautiful but slightly exotic négligé.*

 HELEN *is standing by the window fully dressed, she is holding the curtain aside, and a bar of moonlight comes in to mingle with the amber of the dressing-table lights.* FLORENCE *is obviously extremely hysterical.*

HELEN: Florence, what *is* the use of going on like that?

FLORENCE: I wish I were dead!

HELEN: It's so cowardly to give way utterly – as you're doing.

FLORENCE: I don't care – I don't care!

HELEN: If you don't face things in this world, they only hit you much harder in the end.

FLORENCE: He loved me – he adored me!

HELEN: Never! He hadn't got it in him.

FLORENCE: After all I've done for him, to go to – to Bunty!

HELEN (*leaving the window*): If it hadn't been Bunty it would have been someone else – don't you see how inevitable it was?

FLORENCE: How dared they! – Here! – In this house!

HELEN: That's a little thing, it doesn't matter at all.

FLORENCE: It does – it does —

HELEN: Florence, sit up and pull yourself together.

FLORENCE (*sitting up slowly*): I think I'm going mad.

HELEN: Not a bit of it, you're just thoroughly hysterical.

FLORENCE: Give me some water.

 HELEN *goes to the bathroom and returns with a glass of water.*

FLORENCE (*taking it*): What time is it?

HELEN (*looking at her watch*): Ten-past one.

FLORENCE: Don't go to London by the early train, Helen; stay and come up with me in the car.

HELEN: Very well.

FLORENCE: Thank God, you were here!

HELEN: I wish I'd known what was happening, I might have done something.

FLORENCE: What can I do to get him back?

HELEN: Don't be silly.

FLORENCE: What can I do – what can I do —?

HELEN: Do you mean to say you'd *take* him back after to-night?

FLORENCE: No, never. Not if he crawled to me – never —

HELEN: Well, then, make up your mind definitely never to see him again whatever happens.

FLORENCE: Yes – I will.

HELEN: Why don't you go to bed now?

FLORENCE: I couldn't sleep.

HELEN: Put it all out of your mind – make an effort.

FLORENCE: I can't – I'm too unhappy.

HELEN: Think of Nicky.

FLORENCE: Nicky's young.

HELEN: That doesn't make it any better for him.

FLORENCE: He'll get over it in the long run.

HELEN: The long run never counts at the moment.

FLORENCE: He wasn't in love – really?

HELEN: As much as either you or he are capable of it.

FLORENCE: He's well rid of her – she'd never have appreciated him properly – she hasn't the intelligence.

HELEN: I don't agree with you there – she's got intelligence right enough.

FLORENCE: Treacherous little beast!

HELEN: Yes, but far-seeing.

FLORENCE: Are you standing up for her? Do you think it was *right* of her to get Tom away from me?

HELEN: Yes, quite right.

FLORENCE: Helen!

HELEN: To do her justice, she didn't deliberately set herself out to get him away from you at all. She discovered that in spite of the somewhat decadent years Tom was still her type, and likely to remain so. So with common sense she decided to shelve Nicky forthwith and go for him.

FLORENCE: Her type indeed!

HELEN: Yes, she'd have been quite a nice girl really if she'd been left alone and not allowed to go to Paris and get into the wrong set.

FLORENCE: You are extraordinary, Helen. Do you realise that you're making excuses for the girl who's betrayed your best friend?

HELEN: Don't be so utterly absurd – I'm not making excuses, and anyhow she hasn't betrayed you. She hardly knows you in the first place, and she's just followed her instincts regardless of anyone else's feelings – as you've done thousands of times.

FLORENCE: Helen – you're being horrible to me!

HELEN: I'm not, I'm trying to make you see! You're battering your head against silly cast-iron delusions, and I want to dislodge them.

FLORENCE: Helen, I'm so unhappy – so desperately unhappy.

HELEN: Yes, but not because you've lost Tom, it's something far deeper than that.

FLORENCE: What then?

HELEN: You're on the wrong tack, and have been for years.

FLORENCE: I don't understand.

HELEN: You *won't* understand!

> FLORENCE *gets off the bed and goes over to the dressing-table. She sits and stares at herself in the glass for a moment without speaking.*

FLORENCE: My eyes are sore. (*She powders her face and sprays a little scent on her hair.*) It's so lovely this – and so refreshing.

HELEN: I think I'll go to bed now.

FLORENCE: No, wait a little longer with me – please, Helen – just a few minutes.

HELEN: It's so hot in here.

FLORENCE: Open the window, then.

HELEN: All right.

> *She goes to the window and opens it.* FLORENCE *takes a cigarette out of a box and then shakes a scent-bottle and rubs the cigarette lightly with the stopper.*

FLORENCE: Do you ever do this? It's divine.

HELEN: What a wonderfully clear night – you can see the hills right across the valley – the moon's quite strong.

FLORENCE *goes to the window and stands next to* HELEN *looking out – she is puffing her cigarette.*

FLORENCE: I chose this room in the first place because the view was so lovely.

HELEN: Do you ever look at it?

FLORENCE (*listlessly*): Of course I do, often!

HELEN: It's been raining – I wish you'd throw away that cigarette – it spoils the freshness.

FLORENCE (*turning away*): It's soothing me – calming my nerves.

HELEN: I do wish I could help you – really.

FLORENCE: You are helping me, darling – you're being an angel.

HELEN (*suddenly angry*): Don't talk so emptily, Florence, I'm worth more than that.

FLORENCE: I don't know what you mean.

HELEN: It sickens me to see you getting back so soon.

FLORENCE: Getting back?

HELEN: Yes, to your usual worthless attitude of mind.

FLORENCE: Helen!

HELEN: A little while ago you were really suffering for once, and in a way I was glad because it showed you were capable of a genuine emotion. Now you're glossing it over – smarming it down with your returning vanity, soon you won't be unhappy any more – just vindictive.

FLORENCE: Don't go on at me like that – I'm too wretched.

HELEN (*going to her*): Florence dear, forgive me, but it's true – and I don't want it to be.

The door opens and NICKY *enters. He is in dressing-gown and pyjamas. His face looks strained and white.*

FLORENCE: Nicky!

NICKY: Helen, I want to talk to mother, please.

HELEN: All right, Nicky.

FLORENCE: What is it?

NICKY: I couldn't sleep.

HELEN: Florence dear – good night.

FLORENCE: No – no, Helen – don't go yet —

HELEN: I must.

FLORENCE: Helen – stay with me.

NICKY: Please go.

HELEN: I can't stay, Florence – it's quite impossible.

She goes out.

FLORENCE: I don't know what you mean – by coming here and ordering Helen out of my room.

NICKY: I'm sorry, mother. I felt I had to talk to you alone.

FLORENCE: At this hour of the night – you're mad!

NICKY: No, I'm not, I think I'm probably more unhappy than I've ever been in my life.

FLORENCE: You're young – you'll get over it.

NICKY: I hope so.

FLORENCE: I knew the first moment I saw her – what sort of a girl she was.

NICKY: Oh, mother!

FLORENCE: It's true. I had an *instinct* about her.

NICKY: It's all been rather a shock, you know —

FLORENCE (*becoming motherly*): Yes, dear – I know – I know – but you mustn't be miserable about her – she isn't worth it. (*She goes to kiss him.*)

NICKY (*gently pushing her away*): Don't, mother!

FLORENCE: Listen, Nicky – go back to bed now – there's a dear – my head's splitting.

NICKY: I can't yet.

FLORENCE: Take some aspirin – that'll calm your nerves.

NICKY: I'm afraid I'm a little beyond aspirin.

FLORENCE: I don't want you to think I don't sympathise with you, darling – my heart *aches* for you – I know so well what you're going through.

NICKY: Do you?

FLORENCE: It's agony – absolute agony – but, you see – it will wear off – it always does in time. (NICKY *doesn't answer.*) Nicky, please go now!

NICKY: I want to talk to you.

FLORENCE: To-morrow – we'll talk to-morrow.

NICKY: No, now – *now!*

FLORENCE: You're inconsiderate and cruel – I've told you my head's bursting.

NICKY: I want to sympathise with you, too – and try to understand everything – as well as I can —

FLORENCE: Understand everything?

NICKY: Yes, please.

FLORENCE: I don't know what you mean —

NICKY: Will you tell me things – as though I were somebody quite different?

FLORENCE: What kind of things?

NICKY: Things about you – your life.

FLORENCE: Really, Nicky – you're ridiculous – asking me to tell you stories at this hour!

NICKY (*with dead vehemence*): Mother – sit down quietly. I'm not going out of this room until I've got everything straight in my mind.

FLORENCE (*sinking down – almost hypnotised*): Nicky – please – I —

NICKY: Tom Veryan has been your lover, hasn't he?

FLORENCE (*almost shrieking*): Nicky – how dare you!

NICKY: Keep calm – it's our only chance – keep calm.

FLORENCE (*bursting into tears*): How dare you speak to me like that – suggest such a thing – I —

NICKY: It's true, isn't it?

FLORENCE: Go away – go away!

NICKY: It's true, isn't it?

FLORENCE: No – no!

NICKY: It's true, isn't it?

FLORENCE: No – I tell you – no – no – no!

NICKY: You're lying to me, mother. What's the use of that?

FLORENCE: You're mad – mad —

NICKY: Does father know?

FLORENCE: Go away!

NICKY: Does father know?

FLORENCE: Your father knows nothing – he doesn't understand me any more than you do.

NICKY: Then it's between us alone.

FLORENCE: I tell you I don't know what you're talking about.

NICKY: Mother – don't go on like that, it's useless – we've arrived at a crisis, wherever we go – whatever we do we can't escape from it. I know we're neither of us very strong-minded or capable, and we haven't much hope of coming through successfully – but let's try – it's no good pretending any more

57

– our lives are built up of pretences all the time. For years –
ever since I began to think at all, I've been bolstering up my
illusions about you. People have made remarks not realising
that I was your son, and I've pretended that they were inspired
by cattiness and jealousy. I've noticed things – trivial
incriminating little incidents, and I've brushed them aside and
not thought any more about them because you were my
mother – clever and beautiful and successful – and naturally
people *would* slander you *because* you were so beautiful – and
now I *know* – they were right!

FLORENCE: Nicky – I implore you – go away now – leave me
alone.

NICKY: No, I can't.

FLORENCE: You're cruel – cruel to torment me —

NICKY: I don't want to be cruel —

FLORENCE: Go to bed then, and we'll talk everything over
quietly another time.

NICKY: It is true about Tom Veryan, isn't it?

FLORENCE: No. No —

NICKY: We're on awfully dangerous ground – I'm straining every
nerve to keep myself under control. If you lie to me and try to
evade me any more – I won't be answerable for what might
happen.

FLORENCE (*dropping her voice – terrified*): What do you mean?

NICKY: I don't know – I'm frightened.

FLORENCE: Nicky – darling Nicky – I —

    She approaches him.

NICKY: Don't touch me, please.

FLORENCE: Have a little pity for me.

NICKY: Was Tom Veryan your lover?

FLORENCE (*in a whisper*): Yes.

NICKY: I want to understand why —

FLORENCE: He loved me.

NICKY: But you – did you love him?

FLORENCE: Yes.

NICKY: It was something you couldn't help, wasn't it – something that's always been the same in you since you were quite,
quite young —?

FLORENCE: Yes, Nicky – yes —

NICKY: And there have been others, too, haven't there?

FLORENCE (*with her face in her hands*): I won't be cross-questioned any more – I won't – I won't —

NICKY: I wish you'd understand I'm not blaming you – I'm trying to help you – to help us both —

FLORENCE: What good can all this possibly do?

NICKY: Clear things up, of course. I can't go on any more half knowing —

FLORENCE: Why should that side of my life be any concern of yours?

NICKY: But, mother!

FLORENCE: I'm different from other women – completely different – and you expect me to be the same – why can't you realise that with a temperament like mine it's impossible to live an ordinary humdrum life – you're not a boy any longer – you're a man – and —

NICKY: I'm nothing – I've grown up all wrong.

FLORENCE: It's not my fault.

NICKY: Of course it's your fault, mother – who else's fault *could* it be?

FLORENCE: Your friends – the people you mix with —

NICKY: It wouldn't matter *who* I mixed with if only I had a background.

FLORENCE: You've got as much money as you want – you've got your home —

NICKY (*bitterly*): Home! That's almost funny – there's no peace anywhere – nothing but the ceaseless din of trying to be amused —

FLORENCE: David never complains.

NICKY: I don't suppose you've looked at father during the last few years – or you wouldn't say that.

FLORENCE: He's perfectly happy because he's sensible – he lives his own life and doesn't try to interfere with mine.

NICKY: It must be your vanity that makes you so dreadfully blind – and foolish.

FLORENCE: Understand once and for all, I *won't* be spoken to like this —

NICKY: You've had other lovers besides Tom Veryan – haven't you?

FLORENCE: Yes, I have – I have. Now then!

NICKY: Well, anyhow – that's the truth – at last —

He rises, turns his back on her and stands looking out of the window.

FLORENCE (*after a pause – going to him*): Nicky – don't be angry – please don't be angry with me.

NICKY: I'm not angry a bit – I realise that I'm living in a world where things like this happen – and they've got to be faced and given the right value. If only I'd had the courage to realise everything before – it wouldn't be so bad now – it's the sudden shock that's thrown the whole thing out of focus for me – but I mean to get it right – please help me!

FLORENCE (*dully*): I don't know what to do.

NICKY: It's your life, and you've lived it as you've wanted to live it – that's fair —

FLORENCE: Yes – yes.

NICKY: You've wanted love always – passionate love, because you were made like that – it's not your fault – it's the fault of circumstances and civilisation – civilisation makes rottenness so much easier – we're utterly rotten – both of us —

FLORENCE: Nicky – don't – don't —

NICKY: How can we help ourselves? – We swirl about in a vortex of beastliness – this is a chance – don't you see – to realise the truth – our only chance.

FLORENCE: Oh, Nicky, do stop – go away!

NICKY: Don't keep on telling me to stop when our only hope is to hammer it out.

FLORENCE: You're overwrought – it isn't as bad as you think.

NICKY: Isn't it?

FLORENCE: No, no. Of course it isn't. To-morrow morning you'll see things quite differently.

NICKY: You haven't understood.

FLORENCE: Yes, I have – I have.

NICKY: You haven't understood. Oh, my God, you haven't understood! You're building up silly defences in your mind. I'm overwrought. To-morrow morning I shall see things quite differently. That's true – that's the tragedy of it, and you won't

see – To-morrow morning I *shall* see things differently. All this
will seem unreal – a nightmare – the machinery of our lives
will go on again and gloss over the truth as it always does –
and our chance will be gone for ever.

FLORENCE: Chance – chance? What are you talking about – what
chance?

NICKY: I must make you see somehow.

FLORENCE: You're driving me mad.

NICKY: Have patience with me – please – please —

FLORENCE (*wildly*): How can I have patience with you? – You
exaggerate everything.

NICKY: No I don't – I wish I did.

FLORENCE: Listen – let me explain something to you.

NICKY: Very well – go on.

FLORENCE: You're setting yourself up in judgment on me – your
own mother.

NICKY: No, I'm not.

FLORENCE: You are – you are – let me speak – you don't
understand my temperament in the least – nobody does – I —

NICKY: You're deceiving yourself – your temperament's no
different from thousands of other women, but you've been
weak and selfish and given way all along the line —

FLORENCE: Let me speak, I tell you —!

NICKY: What's the use – you're still pretending – you're building
up barriers between us instead of helping me to break them
down.

FLORENCE: What are you accusing me of having done?

NICKY: Can't you see yet?

FLORENCE: No, I can't. If you're preaching morality you've no
right to – that's my affair – I've never done any harm to
anyone.

NICKY: Look at me.

FLORENCE: Why – what do you mean?

NICKY: You've given me *nothing* all my life – nothing that counts.

FLORENCE: Now you're pitying yourself.

NICKY: Yes, with every reason.

FLORENCE: You're neurotic and ridiculous – just because Bunty broke off your engagement you come and say wicked, cruel things to me —

NICKY: You forget what I've seen to-night, mother.

FLORENCE: I don't care what you've seen.

NICKY: I've seen you make a vulgar, disgusting scene in your own house, and on top of that humiliate yourself before a boy half your age. The misery of losing Bunty faded away when that happened – everything is comparative after all.

FLORENCE: I didn't humiliate myself —

NICKY: You ran after him up the stairs because your vanity wouldn't let you lose him – it isn't that you love him – that would be easier – you never love anyone, you only love them loving you – all your so-called passion and temperament is false – your whole existence had degenerated into an endless empty craving for admiration and flattery – and then you say you've done no harm to anybody – Father used to be a clever man, with a strong will and a capacity for enjoying everything – I can remember him like that, and now he's nothing – a complete nonentity because his spirit's crushed. How could it be otherwise? You've let him down consistently for years – and God knows I'm nothing for him to look forward to – but I might have been if it hadn't been for you —

FLORENCE: Don't talk like that. Don't – don't – it can't be such a crime being loved – it can't be such a crime being happy —

NICKY: You're not happy – you're never happy – you're fighting – fighting all the time to keep your youth and your looks – because you can't bear the thought of living without them – as though they mattered in the end.

FLORENCE (*hysterically*): What does anything matter – ever?

NICKY: That's what I'm trying to find out.

FLORENCE: I'm still young inside – I'm still beautiful – why shouldn't I live my life as I choose?

NICKY: You're not young or beautiful; I'm seeing for the first time how old you are – it's horrible – your silly fair hair – and your face all plastered and painted —

FLORENCE: Nicky – Nicky – stop – stop – stop!

She flings herself face downwards on the bed. NICKY *goes over to her.*

NICKY: Mother!

FLORENCE: Go away – go away – I hate you – go away —

NICKY: Mother – sit up —

FLORENCE (*pulling herself together*): Go out of my room —

NICKY: Mother —

FLORENCE: I don't ever want to see you again – you're insane – you've said wicked, wicked things to me – you've talked to me as though I were a woman off the streets. I can't bear any more – I can't bear any more!

NICKY: I have a slight confession to make —

FLORENCE: Confession?

NICKY: Yes.

FLORENCE: Go away – go away —

NICKY (*taking a small gold box from his pocket*): Look —

FLORENCE: What do you mean – what is it —?

NICKY: Don't you know?

> FLORENCE *takes the box with trembling fingers and opens it. She stares at it for a moment. When she speaks again her voice is quite dead.*

FLORENCE: Nicky, it isn't – you haven't —?

NICKY: Why do you look so shocked?

FLORENCE (*dully*): Oh, my God!

NICKY: What does it matter?

> FLORENCE *suddenly rises and hurls the box out of the window.*

That doesn't make it any better.

FLORENCE (*flinging herself on her knees beside him*): Nicky, promise me, oh, promise you'll never do it again – never in your life – it's frightful – horrible —

NICKY: It's only just the beginning.

FLORENCE: What can I say to you – what can I say to you?

NICKY: Nothing – under the circumstances.

FLORENCE: What do you mean?

NICKY: It can't possibly matter – now.

FLORENCE: Matter – but it's the finish of everything – you're young, you're just starting on your life – you must stop – you must swear never to touch it again – swear to me on your oath, Nicky – I'll help you – I'll help you —

NICKY: You!

63

He turns away.

FLORENCE (*burying her face in her hands and moaning*): Oh – oh – oh!

NICKY: How could you possibly help me?

FLORENCE (*clutching him*): Nicky!

NICKY (*almost losing control*): Shut up – shut up – don't touch me —

FLORENCE (*trying to take him in her arms*): Nicky – Nicky —

NICKY: I'm trying to control myself, but you won't let me – you're an awfully rotten woman, really.

FLORENCE: Nicky – stop – stop – stop —

She beats him with her fists.

NICKY: Leave go of me!

He breaks away from her, and going up to the dressing-table he sweeps everything off on to the floor with his arm.

FLORENCE (*screaming*): Oh – oh – Nicky —!

NICKY: Now then! Now then! You're not to have any more lovers; you're not going to be beautiful and successful ever again – you're going to be my mother for once – it's about time I had one to help me, before I go over the edge altogether —

FLORENCE: Nicky – Nicky —

NICKY: Promise me to be different – you've got to promise me!

FLORENCE (*sinking on to the end of couch, facing audience*): Yes – yes – I promise – (*The tears are running down her face.*)

NICKY: I love you, really – that's why it's so awful.

He falls on his knees by her side and buries his face in her lap.

FLORENCE: No. No, not awful – don't say that – I love you, too.

NICKY (*sobbing hopelessly*): Oh, mother —!

FLORENCE (*staring in front of her*): I wish I were dead!

NICKY: It doesn't matter about death, but it matters terribly about life.

FLORENCE: I know —

NICKY (*desperately*): Promise me you'll be different – promise me you'll be different —

FLORENCE: Yes, yes – I'll try —

NICKY: We'll both try.

FLORENCE: Yes, dear. – Oh, my dear —!

She sits quite still, staring in front of her – the tears are rolling down her cheeks, and she is stroking NICKY'S hair mechanically in an effort to calm him.

CURTAIN

If you enjoy the work of 'The Master', why not join the Noël Coward Society? Members meet on the anniversary of Coward's birthday at the Theatre Royal, Drury Lane to see flowers laid on his statue by a star such as Sir John Mills, Alan Rickman or Vanessa Redgrave. Groups go to Coward productions, places of interest and celebrity meals.

Members receive a free copy of our regular colour magazine, *Home Chat*, as well as discounts on theatre tickets, books and CDs. All are welcome to join – serious students, professional and amateur performers, collectors of memorabilia or simply fans.

Visit our regularly updated website: www.noelcoward.net for a membership form or write to the Membership Secretary:

Noël Coward Society
29 Waldemar Avenue
Hellesdon
Norwich NR6 6TB
UK